"If you are a writer in search of your unique voice, creative authority, and natural way with words, make *How to Be a Writer* the first book you read. Aspiring communicators in any genre will benefit from Barbara's sound, timeless advice on the importance of skill-building, learning by doing, and making the most of the frustration certain to arise along the way. You'll walk away with a more complete understanding of how successful writing happens and how you can tap into your own innate writing ability."

—Christina Katz, author of *Get Known Before the Book Deal* and *Writer Mama*

"Barbara Baig's approach to writing as 'practice and play' makes good sense—and yet we've never heard it before. In strong, clear, humorous prose, Barbara teaches writers skills they can use right away to start making the writing process their own."

—Janet Pocorobba, Assistant Professor and Coordinator, Lesley University MFA Program in Creative Writing

"Barbara Baig's passion for teaching writing infuses every lesson she offers. She demystifies the most complex writing techniques and makes them accessible to all writers."

—Lisa Robinson, M.D., Child Psychiatrist in private practice, Instructor in Psychiatry at Harvard Medical School

"Barbara is a wonderful and inspiring writing teacher, offering clear and helpful suggestions and enthusiastic support! "

—Liz Walker, M.Div., host of *Better Living* on WCVB Television and former CBS4 (WBZ-TV, Boston) news anchor

"I have been writing stories for children for many years and wrote many memoranda and briefs during my career as an attorney, but I still found the course I took from Barbara invaluable to my growth as a writer. Any guide to writing that Barbara authors will be a welcome and well thumbed addition to my bookshelf."

—Laurie A. Jacobs, author, *A Box of Candles*, Winner of the 2005 National Jewish Book Award for Family Literature

"Barbara Baig is that rare writing teacher who has a great deal to offer experienced writers as well as those new to the craft. She inspires students and gives them the tools to hone their craft—no matter what level they begin on."

—Karen Rafinski, award-winning medical and science journalist

"For anyone who worries that writers are born, not made, nothing is more terrifying than a blank page waiting to be filled. Barbara Baig takes the mystery out of the process and shows that, with a little practice and an open mind, good writing can come to anyone."

—Jumana Farouky, former student, now Associate Editor, *TIME* magazine

"Any writer, beginner or experienced, will benefit from reading Barbara Baig's book. She shows us how to develop the skills we need as writers and, best of all, she removes the pressure to produce a finished piece before we are ready. Instead, she invites us to enjoy the freedom of practicing writing in our own time and at our own pace, and she sets out in clear, convincing words how the practice of writing can free up the writer within all of us..."

—Dorothy Stephens, author of *Kwa Heri Means Good-Bye: Memories of Kenya, 1957-59*

"Get ready to take your writing ideas across the finish line by learning the skills and strategies that will give you confidence—and get you practicing."

—Sage Cohen, author of *Writing the Life Poetic* and *The Productive Writer*

HOW TO BE A
writer

*Building Your Creative Skills
Through Practice and Play*

BARBARA BAIG

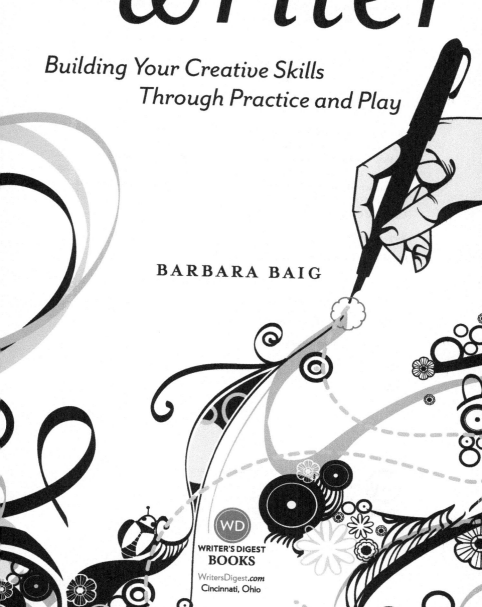

WD
**WRITER'S DIGEST
BOOKS**
WritersDigest.*com*
Cincinnati, Ohio

For more resources for writers, visit www.writersdigest.com/books.

To receive a free weekly e-mail newsletter delivering tips and updates about writing and about Writer's Digest products, register directly at http://newsletters. fwpublications.com.

20 19 18 17 16   11 10 9 8 7

Distributed in Canada by Fraser Direct, 100 Armstrong Avenue, Georgetown, Ontario, Canada L7G 5S4, Tel: (905) 877-4411. Distributed in the U.K. and Europe by F+W Media International, Brunel House, Newton Abbot, Devon, TQ12 4PU, England, Tel: (+44) 1626-323200, Fax: (+44) 1626-323319, E-mail: postmaster@ davidandcharles.co.uk. Distributed in Australia by Capricorn Link, P.O. Box 704, Windsor, NSW 2756 Australia, Tel: (02) 4577-3555.

Library of Congress Cataloging-in-Publication Data

Baig, Barbara.

How to be a writer / by Barbara Baig. -- 1st ed.

p. cm.

Includes bibliographical references and index.

ISBN 978-1-58297-805-5 (pbk. : alk. paper)

1. Authorship--Vocational guidance. I. Title.

PN147.B25 2010

808'.02023--dc22

2009044790

Edited by Kelly Nickell and Scott Francis
Designed by Claudean Wheeler
Cover illustration by Natasha R. Graham/ iStockphoto
Production coordinated by Debbie Thomas

About the Author

Barbara Baig has devoted herself for almost three decades to the practices of writing and teaching. She has conducted dozens of writing workshops and classes for adults and college students, and was the writing instructor at Harvard Divinity School for twenty years. She now teaches in the MFA Program in Creative Writing at Lesley University.

Her website is www.wherewriterslearn.com

Table of Contents

Welcome

When many people write, they struggle and suffer. Perhaps you are one of them: If so, this book is for you.

Or perhaps you love to write and want to get better at it. This book is for you, too.

Or perhaps you long to explore the world of "creative writing" but aren't sure where to begin. This book is for you as well.

This book is a guide to the basics of writing—a very different kind of guide from other writing books. It will not give you strategies for getting published, nor will it show you techniques for digging deep into your psyche. It will not teach you grammar or how to write a best-selling novel. Instead it will show you how to develop certain basic and essential skills that all writers need, whether they are just beginning to write or have gotten blocked or confused somewhere along the way.

What sets this book apart is that it sees writing as a certain kind of work, work that *anyone* can learn how to do, and to do well. You don't need some magical quality called "talent" or "inspiration"; you need *skills*. Unfortunately, these skills are rarely taught in school, or even in most writing workshops. So when many people sit down to write, they are held back because they simply don't have the skills they need. And then they usually blame themselves: *I don't have any talent. I must be stupid.* But the fault is not theirs; the fault

lies with an educational system that has not provided them with the basic skills they need to do a writer's work.

Many people are also held back from developing their abilities as writers because of a pervading myth that the only "real" writers are those who are born with the skills they need. That's nonsense. Writing skills can be acquired by anyone who is willing to put time and energy into the process of acquiring them. You don't have to be born with writing skills: You can *learn* them. This book will show you how to do that.

THE REAL WORK OF WRITING

When we learn how to write, though, what exactly is it that we are learning? Answers to this question differ. Some people believe that all we need to learn are grammar and spelling, rules and formulas. Other people say that writing is thinking on paper. Still others are convinced that learning to write means "freeing your creativity" or "expressing yourself." I take yet another approach, one that I believe is both comprehensive and practical.

To write is to do a certain kind of work: the work of communication on paper. Skilled writers, in any genre, do not see themselves as producing texts—that's merely the academic view of writing. Nor do they see themselves as engaging only in self-expression; to light a candle, play some soothing music, and let the words flow can indeed be therapeutic, but it's unlikely to produce writing that anyone else will want to read. No matter what kind of writing they do, skilled writers see themselves as communicators; they have something to say, and they want to get that "something" into the minds of their readers.

As with any activity, if you want to do the work of writing, you need particular skills. A baseball player who wants to become a good hitter needs to know how to keep his eye on the pitched ball and how to swing the bat properly. A pianist needs to know how to read music and move her fingers over the keyboard. Just like athletes or musicians, writers need particular skills.

First, writers need to know how to come up with content for a piece of writing. They need to be able to find subjects to write about and to discover the things they want to say about those subjects. No matter what kind of writing you are doing, whether it be a short story or a poem or an office memo, it must have content.

Second, writers need to be able to consider their readers. Skilled writers know how to grab their readers' attention and keep it, from the beginning of a piece to the end. They know how to make what they have to say clear to their readers; they know how to affect them, to make them laugh, or cry, or think. Skilled writers understand, and know how to make use of, what I call the natural relationship between writer and reader.

Third, writers need to know the form, or genre, they want to use to communicate. A novel works differently from a poem; a business report works differently from a short story. Skilled writers have a command of their chosen form.

Finally, writers need the ability to use language to get what's in their own minds (and, if appropriate, their hearts) into the minds (and hearts) of their readers. Skilled writers know how to use words and sentences and paragraphs to *transfer* material from their own minds into the minds of other people. And they also know how to use language to make things happen inside their readers, to make them laugh or cry, to inform them, to persuade them, to teach.

I have said that skilled writers "know" these things. But I hasten to point out that no writer, whatever his or her level of skill, was born with this knowledge. The skills we need to communicate well on paper are primarily *learned* skills. If you struggle to write, most likely that's because you were never given the opportunity to learn these skills.

In this book, I give you that opportunity for the first two skills (coming up with things to say and considering readers). I call these "content" skills, and in the chapters that follow you will learn, first, how to exercise and develop the faculties that enable you to come up with content for a piece of writing, and then, how to establish a natural relationship with your readers so that you can pass on that content to them, through the medium of your chosen genre.

This book does not give instruction in how to write in particular forms; there are hundreds of books available that will teach you how to write a novel or a poem or a business letter. Nor do I cover the craft of writing here. That's because there's so much to learn about how to choose words and put them together into sentences and paragraphs that I decided to write another book (now in progress) to teach these particular skills.

You might find it odd that a book about writing does not include instruction about genre and craft. Perhaps you wonder, *Isn't writing all about using words?*

Yes, it is indeed true that skillful writing demands the ability to use language well—and, at the same time, it also demands the other skills I have described. People who are good writers are good, not simply because they can craft elegant sentences, but because they have something to say and because they know how to be in appropriate relationship to their readers. My experiences as a teacher have shown me that when I am reading a piece of writing that is weak or confusing—whether it be an academic paper, a short story, a business speech, or a poem—it's not usually because the writer lacks language (though that is sometimes the case); it's because he or she didn't know how to come up with and develop content. After all, it's pretty hard to write well if you have nothing to say! Skilled writers grab and keep the attention of readers, not just with words but with *content* —ideas or information, scenes or characters.

There's another reason I have chosen to teach only content skills in this book: The best way to learn a complex activity is to break it down into its component parts and then practice each one of those skills separately. When an aspiring baseball player learns to hit a ball, he might take hundreds of swings in practice focusing entirely on keeping his eye on the ball, and hundreds more focusing on keeping his wrists level. The same thing is true when someone learns to play a musical instrument, like the piano: A beginner might practice a piece many times using only her left hand, then many more using only her right hand. The best way to learn how to write is, I believe, to follow this model: to put all one's attention into learning first one skill, then another, then another, and so on. Finally, just as a batter eventually learns to keep his eye on the ball and keep his wrists level at the same time, and a pianist plays her piece with both hands at once, a trained writer becomes able to use all of a writer's skills.

The key to learning skills, whether one is an athlete, a musician, or a writer, is practice. No matter your age, no matter your cultural and educational background, if you are willing to practice, you can acquire these skills. All you need is desire, and some time to practice.

WRITING AS A LEARNING JOURNEY

My approach to writing has this belief at its core: To become a more accomplished, more confident writer is to take a learning journey. Learning through practice —repeating an activity over and over—has always been one of the main ways that humans learn; just remember how you learned to walk or to drive a car. To be on a learning journey as a writer means that you move forward from one place to another, taking steps one at a time to build your skills and your understanding of what you are doing.

You can embark on this learning journey with a particular goal in mind. Perhaps you want to write and publish a novel or a memoir or a collection of poems. The practices in this book will give you a solid foundation of skills and understanding from which you can then proceed to learn more about your chosen genre.

You need not have such a goal, though. You can choose to take a learning journey as a writer, to engage in the practice of writing, for the sake of the journey and the practice alone. The benefits of writing practice are the same whether you aim to become a professional writer or prefer to be an amateur.

Those benefits are considerable. The practice of writing keeps your mental faculties exercised, and so it is good for your brain, just as working out or playing tennis regularly is good for your body. Writing practice keeps your brain awake and alive; it improves your ability to concentrate. Whether or not you ever publish a thing, regular writing practice will give you skills you can use in your work and your personal life, and make you feel more empowered. It will improve your ability to communicate, stimulate your curiosity, and make you more aware of the world around you and the world of your imagination. Writing practice will also increase your enjoyment of what you read, because the more you practice, the more you will understand what professional writers are doing in their work.

The discipline of a writing practice will help you complete writing projects, and it can be transferred to other areas of your life. Writing practice, like any regular practice, provides a focus for your energies, a way to center and ground yourself. It can substitute for, or be an adjunct to, any other practice you enjoy, such as meditation or running.

When you learn, through practice, how to be a better writer, you can benefit others as well. Right now, people who can communicate on paper seem to be in rather short supply. The damage done by bad writing can be found just about everywhere: from the poorly written office e-mail that confuses its recipients, to the unintelligible directions that come with the latest gadget, to the accident at the Three Mile Island nuclear plant, caused, some say, by a badly written memo. Our world *needs* people who can communicate clearly and powerfully, imaginatively and passionately, through the written word.

Most of all, to become a practicing writer sets your feet on a path of lifelong learning. To write is, beyond everything, to be a learner, someone who is constantly discovering new things—about writing, about the world, about life. The discoveries you will make on your journey as a practicing writer are yours alone, a treasure that no one can ever take from you.

So while the practices in this book are certainly tools for developing writing skills, for training your writing "muscles," they are also tools for learning—not school-based learning, but real learning—learning that can help you discover your genuine interests and your own path on this planet.

HOW TO USE THIS BOOK

There are two main kinds of writing: writing we want to do, and writing we have to do. In neither case can we rely on inspiration alone; we need well-trained writing muscles and an understanding of the work of writing. This book will provide you with a practice field where you can train these muscles—I prefer to call them a writer's powers—and it will give you an understanding of the process of taking a piece of required writing from initial idea to finished product.

If what you need right now is to get something written, then the section called *Required Writing* will guide you, step-by-step, through that process. If you are writing something for which you have a deadline, then you will want to turn to that section first. Here I help you overcome fears and anxieties about writing by making clear what you actually have to *do* to get from a vague idea in your mind to a finished piece of writing that communicates what you want to say to your intended audience. You will learn how to generate and develop ideas, how to avoid procrastination and use your time effectively, how to think about your audience and purpose, how to organize, and how to revise.

If, though, you are coming to this book because you love to write (or because you want to find or recover that desire within yourself), and if you have time to explore the world of writing without deadlines, then I invite you to move at your own pace through the chapters that follow. They will show you some fundamental tools you can use to learn writing skills. They will also introduce you to the mental faculties writers use to develop content for pieces of writing—creativity, memory and expertise, observation, imagination, curiosity, the subconscious—and they will show you ways to train these faculties so that you will be able to come up with ideas and material for pieces of writing anytime you want to. Other chapters will teach you to grow a piece of writing; that is, to develop its content beyond your initial ideas. You will also learn how to establish a natural relationship with your readers and how to practice using that relationship as you write, so that you can find your own voice on the page and communicate clearly and powerfully.

The practices in this book will be of use to you for any kind of writing you want to do, be it nonfiction or fiction, poetry or memoir. Done faithfully, these practices will build your skills and bring you pleasure in writing; they will give you the confidence that comes with knowing what you are doing when you write; they may even change your life.

I have organized this book as much like a workshop as possible, so you will probably get the most benefit from it by beginning at the beginning. If you prefer, though, you can certainly start with whatever piece looks most interesting to you: Everything in the book is, at the deepest level, connected to everything else.

My workshops are always hands-on: There really isn't any way to learn about writing just by listening to someone talk about it. You have to *do* it. This book takes the same approach: Certainly you can benefit by simply reading through it. But if you really want to become a better, more confident writer, you need to practice, just as you would if you wanted to become a better basketball player or a better pianist.

I would never assume that I know everything that there is to know about writing or about teaching writing. For me, teaching, like writing itself, is a learning journey. As I do my own work, and guide others to do theirs, I continue to learn more about both activities. For years my students have been asking me to put what I teach them into a book; and here it is.

Welcome to the journey.

SECTION 1
getting started

CHAPTER 1

What Is Writing Practice (and How Do I Do It)?

Two musicians are walking down the street on the West Side of New York City. A little old lady approaches and asks them politely, "Could you gentlemen tell me how to get to Carnegie Hall?" The musicians look at each other and exchange knowing grins. Then one of them turns to her and says, "Practice! Practice!"

Everyone knows that aspiring musicians need to practice. They practice to learn their skills; they practice to keep those skills sharp. Vladimir Horowitz, the world-famous pianist, said, "I practice every day. If I don't practice for one day, I know it. If I don't practice for two days, the critics know it. If I don't practice for three days, the audience knows it."

Anyone who follows professional sports knows that athletes don't just go out and play games; they practice for hours every day. Larry Bird, who became a star basketball player for the Boston Celtics, started out on his career in high school by going to the gym at 6 A.M. every day to practice; among other things, he took five hundred free throws a day. We all take for granted that a kid who wants to hit home runs like David Ortiz in his prime has to devote years to hitting practice, or that one who wants to play guitar like Eric Clapton has to put in a lot of hours with her instrument before she can play cosmic blues riffs.

But writers? Surely they don't need to practice. After all, aren't all good writers simply born with their talent?

Yes, some people are born with an aptitude for writing, just as some are born with an aptitude for playing the piano or hitting a fastball. But even people who have a talent for some activity must develop that talent. And when it comes to writing, many people who believe (or have been told) they can't write are, in fact, perfectly capable of learning how.

This idea that only certain special people can write is one of the great myths about writing. If you have been paralyzed by that myth, I urge you to abandon it right now. Writing, like sports or music, is something just about anyone can learn how to do. The most important word in that last sentence is the word *learn*. If you are willing to put some time and energy into the work of learning to write, you can most definitely become a better writer.

And the key to this learning is the activity of practice.

WHY YOU'VE NEVER PRACTICED WRITING

Everyone accepts that athletes and musicians learn their skills and keep them honed through practice. Anyone who suggested that the Red Sox, for instance, should just go play games without ever practicing would be laughed at. The same goes for a musician who decided to rent Carnegie Hall to give a piano recital without ever practicing the pieces she planned to play. We accept that if someone is going to undertake a public performance—on an athletic field, or in a concert—she has to build her skills and prepare herself through practice.

A finished piece of writing, one that other people are going to read, is just as much a performance as a baseball game or a recital. You, like most adults in this culture, have turned out hundreds of such pieces, in school or at work. How much practice time were you given to develop your skills before you had to perform on the page?

Chances are very good that your answer is: "little or none."

That's because most of us who are now adults learned how to write in school, and that means our writing was done under performance conditions—it always counted. Every essay, every book report, every poem or story was graded, if not by itself, then as part of a portfolio of work. If you had a typical American education, you were expected to produce finished pieces of writing without ever having had an opportunity to do any practice writing.

Even if your writing education has taken place in creative writing workshops, you may also be a victim of the "performance" approach, for most workshops and creative writing classes are also performance-oriented. Here the performance demands are different from those students face in academic classes: The goal is not grades but publication. Participants in these workshops critique each other's writing based on the (often unspoken) assumption that every piece must be—or become—of publishable quality, or it's a failure.

There are serious consequences to this approach to writing instruction. First, as a result of this approach, many adults assume that writing is different from sports or music: Somehow we should be able to just do it. *Either you've got the gift*, we conclude, *or you don't*. Even more important, it's almost impossible to learn skills under performance conditions; we're too anxious, too focused on the result. When we know our writing is going to be judged, we can't relax as we write. And if we can't relax, then we can't truly learn.

And there's one more reason why so many adults feel blocked or baffled or downright terrified when they sit down to write: They have no idea what they are supposed to be doing.

That's because the writing instruction most adults got in school was focused on the characteristics of the finished product, rather than the skills needed to produce it. The minds of most adults are cluttered with instructions about what a finished piece of writing should look like—whether it's "introduction-body-conclusion" or "avoid comma splices" or "show don't tell"—and empty of any clear understanding of how to produce that piece of writing in the first place. No one has ever taken apart the activity of writing for them—the way a hitting coach, for instance, might take apart the activity of swinging at a baseball—and shown them its component skills. No one has ever given them an opportunity to practice those component skills so that, when they are in a performance situation of wanting to make a poem or a story (or having to produce a report at work) they have the training to do it.

Fortunately, the good news is that it's never too late to learn writing skills through practice.

WHAT IS WRITING PRACTICE?

Writing practice, like batting practice or practicing scales, is the repetition of an activity over and over to develop certain skills. An athlete needs to develop hand-eye coordination, for example; a musician needs to develop her ear. Writers, as I've said, need to develop a wide range of skills, from coming up with content to finding the words to communicate what they have to say. When we do writing practice, we are training and building our brains in certain ways, just as athletes train their muscles. Then, when we are in a performance situation, we can rely on our skills to serve us.

Writing practice is not merely mindless repetition, though. When an aspiring baseball player practices hitting, he's not just swinging the bat over and over; he's swinging the bat and putting his attention into one thing at a time. He might, for instance, take a number of swings concentrating all his attention on gripping the bat properly; he might take more swings concentrating on keeping his eye on the ball. This same directing of attention to one thing at a time, when we practice putting words on paper, is also the essence of writing practice.

It's essential to concentrate on one thing at a time when we practice because writing, like hitting a baseball, is a complex skill. When we devote all of our attention to one part of it—say, coming up with things to say—we strengthen the part of our minds that does that particular thing. Then, when we sit down to write a piece for others to read, we have trained writing muscles to make use of.

Writing practice is not difficult; anyone, no matter his or her level of skill with writing, can do it. The most important thing to remember is that, in deciding to build your skills through practice, you are giving up having to be a performing writer. Instead, you are letting yourself be a practicing writer.

Here are some ways to do that.

Forget What You've Learned

If you are one of those people whose head has been stuffed full of rules about writing (many of them probably contradicting each other), then try to let go of them while you are practicing. They will only get in your way. Once you've established your skills, you can then revisit the rules and decide which ones you want to make use of.

If, as a result of writing under performance conditions, you find yourself getting tense as you approach practice, try to relax. It's only practice!

Don't Treat Practice Like School

Many people automatically put themselves into the mind-set of being in school when they begin to do writing practices: They want to know whether they are doing everything "right."

It's not surprising that this should occur: We are used to thinking of being in school as the only possible way to learn. To engage in regular writing practice, though, is to step outside the confines of school learning, with its requirements and tests and grades, into a realm where you are free to learn in your own way. You can learn at your own pace, and you can decide what you want to be learning at any particular time.

Make a Safe Place for Your Practice

Becoming a practicing writer gives you the freedom to learn in your own way because writing practice is always private. When you write in school (or at work) your writing is always going to be read by someone: It's public writing. But no one need ever see a word of your practice writing unless you choose to share it. This privacy gives you a safe place to learn: You can experiment and let yourself adventure in the world of writing. (One advantage to practicing writing rather than a musical instrument like the drums or the saxophone, or practicing a sport, is that no one can see or hear us while we practice!) While our ultimate goal as writers is communication, having the opportunity to practice in private gives us the opportunity to heal from bad experiences we may have had.

I am always amazed by the horror stories people tell me about their experiences with writing: I've heard about teachers who mock student writing in class and about bosses who literally rip to shreds a subordinate's memo. One woman in a class I taught said that whenever she wrote a letter to her mother, her mother would send it back with all the grammatical errors circled in red. I thought that was a uniquely horrible experience—until other students told me the same thing had happened to them.

Far more people than you might imagine have had experiences like this. Such experiences hurt. Even worse, they undermine our confidence as writers. Worst of all, we internalize those negative responses to our writing and adopt a very judgmental attitude toward our own words on the page. Even people whose writing has been praised can adopt this judgmental attitude: *This isn't as good as what I wrote last time. I guess I don't have it any more.*

Many people find it hard, at first, to take in fully that the writing they do during practice sessions will not be judged by anyone; after years of writing in school, they retain a kind of inner teacher who lies in wait to pounce upon their writing and red-pencil all the mistakes. It can take a while to realize that when you are doing writing practice, there *are* no mistakes. It's very difficult to do any of these practices wrong; they are designed to be open-ended and flexible so that when you do them you can learn something about writing or about yourself as a writer.

So, as you do the writing practices, let go of that judgmental part of your mind. You are learning new things here. Be kind and gentle and patient with yourself, as you would be with a child learning to walk. Give yourself lots of encouragement: *I practiced today! That's great!*

GIVE YOURSELF TIME FOR PRACTICE

Practice is a way to learn that is very different from the kind of learning we must do in school or at work. There we must rush through every assignment, trying to get it in by the deadline. But in practice there are no deadlines; there is only getting up the next day and doing more practicing. Practice makes possible slow—and thorough—learning.

Remember, too, that it takes time to learn how to become a writer, or a better one; there's a lot to learn, and not everyone learns in the same way, or at the same pace. Don't push yourself to keep up with others.

In school we are often forced to move on to the next thing before we have fully understood what we are trying to learn now.

That's in part because there the path of learning is assumed to be a straight line: curricula, whether in elementary school or university, are planned to move students always forward, from elementary arithmetic to calculus, for instance, or from introductory sociology to advanced.

But when we undertake learning through practice, we are not walking a linear path. Instead, we are engaging in what I like to call spiral learning.

ENGAGE IN SPIRAL LEARNING

Picture a straight line; then picture a spiral. Now imagine walking along that straight line, and then walking along the spiral. In both cases, you will be moving forward, but in the case of the spiral, your forward movement will depend on also continuously going around in a circle. It sounds like a paradox; but, in fact, it is the best possible way to learn—and it is the way of learning made possible through practice. When we do the same thing over and over in practice, we are essentially making a circle. But at the same time, every time we repeat a practice, we have the opportunity to learn something new, to move forward in our understanding of what we are doing.

Here's an example: In the t'ai chi class I attend, we do "the form"—a series of connected movements designed by one of the twentieth-century t'ai chi masters. The form is always the same. We may do it in different ways to practice it differently, but the movements never change. I have been studying t'ai chi for ten years; my teacher, Peter Wayne, has been studying, and doing this same form, for over thirty. Almost every time I do the form, I learn something. Often it is something I learned at an earlier point in my study but have forgotten, or now understand in a new way.

The writing practices I present in this book have been inspired, in part, by what I have learned from t'ai chi. They provide you with an opportunity to learn by doing, to learn through experience. You can return to each of them, over and over, through years of becoming a writer, and you can learn more deeply and more fully what it has to teach you. So give yourself a chance to do the practices more than once—they are all designed to be repeated—and to come back to them again and again as you need to. You will find that every time you return to a practice and do it for a while, you will learn something new.

LET GO OF EXPECTATIONS

Practice is a tool for learning. Its goal is not to produce finished products. So when you practice, try to let go of the part of your mind that focuses on results. The improvements in your writing that will come to you through practice will not come all at once, and they won't come at all if you are constantly putting pressure on yourself to produce a finished piece.

These practices are really just little games for grown-ups. Have fun with them. Give up the judgmental attitude you probably learned in school: *Is this any good?* Instead, say to yourself: *I wonder what will happen when I try THIS?* Just notice what happens to come out onto the page this time when you do a particular exercise. Next time, something different may happen.

Taking note, without judgment, of what happens when you do a practice, is the best way I know to set your feet firmly on your own learning path as a writer. When you simply notice the words you have put on the page, rather than compare them to writing you imagine is better or worse, then you can decide what it is in those words, or in the way they came to you, that you like and want to spend more time with.

I also urge you not to come to your practice with the attitude of "I must do this," or add writing practice to the long list of *shoulds* in your life. While you may find that, as with exercise, it takes a little while for you to establish the habit of practicing, let yourself sit down to write because you want to, because you enjoy doing it, because you want to fool around with ideas and images. Let your practice be your own private playground where you can swing or run or slide to your heart's content.

LET YOURSELF PLAY!

Some of you may have negative associations with the word *practice*. Perhaps, as a child, you were forced into playing scales when you wanted to be outside; or perhaps you had to endure too many drills during football practices. But writing practice is not merely mindless repetition. Above all, writing practice is play!

To let yourself play as you do the practices initiates a process of learning through discovery: You will find out what you need to learn next, not what someone else thinks you should learn. Such self-directed learning is an adventure that can be as satisfying and thrilling as first learning to walk. And so, as I tell my students in class, if you need someone to give you permission to play, I give it to you now!

GIVE WRITING PRACTICE A TRY

Take a pen and a piece of paper. (If you prefer, use your computer.) Set a timer for ten minutes, or put a clock or a watch beside you so you can glance at it but not stare at it. Take a few deep breaths to relax yourself. Then pick up the pen and write. You can write anything. You don't have to have a subject. If you happen to wander into a subject, you don't have to stay there. You don't have to be organized. You don't have to compose coherent sentences and paragraphs. You don't have to spell words correctly. You don't even have to make sense. No one will ever see this. You don't even have to read it over if you don't want to; you can just tear it up and throw it away.

The only thing you have to do is to keep the pen moving no matter what. That means no stopping to think, no going back to cross out or change a word. You can write the same thing over and over again, until your mind gives you something else. You can write, "This is so dumb! I can't believe I'm doing this." It doesn't matter what you write. Just keep the pen moving.

You don't have to write fast. And you don't have to clutch the pen in a grip like a gorilla's. (That will only make your hand hurt.)

Ready? Take those few deep, relaxing breaths. Go!

When your ten minutes (or more, if you like) are up, bring the writing to a close.

Congratulations! You are now a real writer.

My students always laugh when I say this after the first time they do this exercise (usually called freewriting[1]). But then I go on to tell them that I'm not joking: A real writer is someone who really writes. Not someone who thinks about it. Not someone who talks about it. But someone who puts words on the page, one after another after another. At the most fundamental level, this is what it means to be a writer: putting words on the page is what writers do. You probably won't want to show anyone these particular words. You may not even want to read them over yourself. That doesn't matter. What matters is that, for the last ten minutes or so, you were practicing being a writer.

Now, take another few minutes—as long as you like—to reflect, on paper, about what happened as you did this exercise. What did you notice about the words that came to you, or how they came to you; what did you notice in yourself as you wrote?

There are no right or wrong answers to these questions. Often beginning writers will comment on how free they felt as they wrote. Some will be amazed at how their minds kept giving them new things to write about. Others are equally surprised by how deeply they were able to go into one subject, often something they had been thinking about for some time. When I ask, "Is this different from what usually happens when you write?" most people will reply: "Yes!"

THE PURPOSE OF FREEWRITING PRACTICE

What is going on here? To understand this, we need to understand something about the activity of writing. When we write, we need to use two different mental faculties: one, which we can call the "creative faculty," is the part of the mind that comes up with things to say, with ideas and images and words; the other—let's call it the "critical faculty"—is the part of the mind that evaluates those words and ideas.

Most of us were taught to write by following a model of the writing process I call the "one-step"—or the "get-it-right-the-first-time"—model. According to this model, first you figure out what you want to say, then you make an outline, and then you sit down to write. And as you write, what comes out onto the page should be as close to perfect as you can get it. For some writers this model works; for most of us, though, it doesn't work at all—and when it doesn't, we figure that we just can't write, or we're stupid, or possibly both.

But why doesn't this model work? When you are trying to get your writing to be "right" the first time, you are forced to use your creative faculty and your critical faculty at the same time. This is a difficult and often dangerous thing to do, because the two faculties can get in each other's way and paralyze you. For instance, your creative faculty says, "Hey, I've got this great idea!" and you start to write it down. But immediately your critical faculty jumps in and says things like, "Oh, that idea will never work," or "You can't say that!" or "That sentence is ungrammatical," or any other of the many things that our critical faculties have been trained to say. And then what happens is a mental short circuit—everything jams, and you end up staring at the page or out the window; you decide that this is a great time to get some coffee or do the laundry or walk the dog—or anything except write.

It's not that the creative faculty is the good guy, and the critical faculty is the bad guy; as writers, we need both of these faculties. The block happens when we are following the one-step model and so are being forced to use both faculties at the same time.

A number of years ago, teachers of writing began to study how professional writers work; they learned that many of these writers do not follow the one-step model or try to achieve perfection on a first draft. Instead they see writing, not as something that happens all at once, but as something that happens in stages. For these writers, the work of writing is a process. And because they are not trying to end up with a finished piece of writing in one giant step, they are able to use the creative faculty and the critical faculty separately, at different times as they work.

When you can do this—and it's easy to learn to do—then you can get the most out of each of your faculties, both the creative one and the critical one.

At this point you might be thinking, *I don't have a creative faculty.* Oh, yes, you do! When I use the word *creative* here, I am not talking about imaginative genres of writing, like fiction or poetry; I mean simply the ability to come up with things to say and the words to say them. We are born with this faculty. Unfortunately, many of us are denied access to it by an educational system largely devoted to tests and grades. But even if your creative faculty has been lying dormant for many years, you can awaken it.

That's what the practice you just tried will do. Freewriting is practice for your creative faculty, to strengthen it and help you become comfortable using it. Most people who have spent a long time in school have very well-developed critical faculties and pathetically underdeveloped creative faculties. For any writer, of any kind of writing, this is a serious problem. For it's the creative faculty, not the critical faculty, that comes up with things to say and the words to say them. And while your junior high English teacher may have deducted marks for spelling and grammar mistakes and ignored the content of your papers, the truth is that, unless your work has interesting content, no one will voluntarily read it. (Teachers don't count: They are required to read their students' writing, no matter how bad it is.) I am not suggesting that spelling and grammar are not important; certainly, they are. But they are important because they are conventions, and if you don't follow them, your reader will be distracted and confused and will not stay focused on what you are saying. By themselves, they will never make a good piece of writing.

Freewriting is like aerobics for your creative faculty. Because you cannot stop, and because you know no one will ever read what you write, you are free to let your creative faculty run around and play. And play it certainly will. It will give you ideas, it will give you words, it will give you questions. It will make leaps and take you places you never expected to go. (It will, quite often, also give you junk.)

The key to this practice is to have no expectations at all. It doesn't matter what you write. The point of the practice is the doing of the practice, not the immediate results. Over time, and with regular practice, you will strengthen your creative faculty, just as lifting weights will strengthen your muscles.

If you have spent a lot of time writing for critical teachers or bosses, you may find that you have a lot of voices in your head telling you all the things you should or shouldn't do on the page, or judging your thoughts or ideas. The more you practice, the more you will be able to let go of these voices. As you let them go, you will open up your mind more and more to your own ideas and words.

This doesn't mean that everything you put down on the page during a practice session is brilliant—far from it! But it's very often the case that we criticize our own words and ideas too quickly, that we shut the door on potentially useful material. Instead, try to follow this advice from the American poet William Stafford: "The correct attitude to have towards any words that come to you is, 'Welcome, welcome.'" When you practice, let your paper (or computer screen) invite your words with an echo of Stafford's: *Welcome. Welcome.*

WAYS TO USE FREEWRITING

Throughout this book you will learn many different ways to use the tool of freewriting. At the beginning, though, I think it's essential to just do lots of this basic practice. As with any other form of exercise, start small. If you want to get into better physical shape, it's much better to go for a short walk every day than to hike a mountain once every six months; the same principle holds for strengthening your creative faculty. Try doing freewriting practice for a minimum of ten minutes three times a week, for a few weeks. See what happens. Perhaps after a while you will want to practice every day.

You can do this practice as an independent activity, or you can use it to help you do other things. Perhaps you'd like to use it at work to settle your mind when you arrive or to jot down your tasks for the day. Perhaps you'd like to use it to vent anger at a person you are unable to talk with about your feelings. Freewriting is also a great way to warm up and get into "writing gear" before you write something you have to write; it's much easier to get started on that required writing when you've already been putting words on the page for ten minutes. You can use freewriting to keep a journal (as long as you keep your pen moving) or to write letters to friends. As you experiment, you may discover other ways to make the practice part of your life.

Can you freewrite on the computer? Certainly, if you wish. But you need to be careful that you don't start changing things and editing as you go along. It's important not to look at the words as they are coming out on the screen. Look at your fingers or out the window, or cover the screen with a piece of paper.

GUIDELINES FOR FREEWRITING

Keep the pen moving, no matter what, for a minimum of ten minutes. Try not to look at your watch. Set an alarm or a timer instead.

If you find yourself wanting to stop, don't give in to that impulse. Just notice it, and keep the pen moving, even if you have to repeat what you just wrote over and over until you think of something else to say. If you write something and then think of another way to say it, write down those new words without editing or crossing out the old ones.

Make sure that you keep this writing absolutely private. You must feel safe to write whatever you want.

You can start with a subject, if you want to, but you don't have to. And if you start writing about one subject, you can switch to another, and another ...and another. Just keep the pen moving. Don't worry about order or word choice or grammatical correctness. No one will see this.

If you find yourself wandering into territory that you don't want to explore, just change direction. You are in charge of this practice.

Have no expectations for this writing. You might get something you like; you might not. It doesn't matter. Try to take this attitude: "I wonder what ideas or images will come to me this time?"

Put your attention into listening to the words and ideas that come to you and putting them down on the page. If you hear voices in your mind telling you things like, "This is awful! Whatever made you think you could write?" or "Wow! This is great! You'll be the next Stephen King!" just ignore them. Keep your pen moving.

How to Be a Writer

You may find it best, in the beginning, not to read over what you have written. If you do want to read it, it's helpful to wait a little while before you do. And be sure to read it over in a benign spirit. Don't edit it or critique it; just notice what is there and what you like.

THE BENEFITS OF FREEWRITING

The most important benefit you will derive from the practice of freewriting is to become comfortable putting thoughts and words on the page without getting in your own way. You will become more comfortable with the activity of writing. You will also learn that your creative faculty always has something to give you. It may not give you great ideas; it may give you nothing but questions or complaints or wonderings about what to make for dinner—but there will always be something it has to give. Taking this in, you will, I hope, begin to feel more confidence in the ability of your mind to come up with things to say.

Freewriting can also dramatically improve your ability to concentrate. Many of us are distracted when we write by all the other voices in our heads: not only the chorus of judging voices, but also voices nattering at us about other things that we should be doing or what we should or shouldn't have said to so-and-so. With freewriting, as you learn to give more of your attention to the thoughts that are coming to you, those other voices can fade out. This means that eventually, with lots of practice, you will be able to write more efficiently.

Freewriting is also a wonderful technique to help you examine your feelings or think through a problem on paper. Even more important, it's an amazingly powerful learning tool.

Freewriting is not finished writing. You are not going to send out your freewriting to be published or necessarily show it to anyone. Freewriting is a practice, like practicing scales or fielding grounders; when undertaken in this way, it will help you become a better writer.

This basic practice is deceptively simple. Don't be fooled by its simplicity. You can learn a great deal from doing it. Most of all, regular practice will instill in you the attitude of putting words on paper without getting in your own way. That is the foundation for any kind of writing you want (or are required) to do.

THE JOY OF PRACTICE

At the same time, while practice will certainly build your skills, you can, if you like, engage in it with no other goal than the doing of the practice. I urge you to remember that you can do the writing practices simply because you enjoy them. You don't have to "get someplace" with your writing. Just as you don't have to be a professional pianist to enjoy playing the piano and taking lessons, or a professional basketball player to enjoy a Saturday afternoon game with your friends, so too you can sit down to practice writing because this is a way you like to spend your time.

You don't have to be, or to become, a great writer to have a wonderful, fulfilling, and transformative writing practice. I have been practicing t'ai chi for many years, almost every day, and I'm still not very good at it—but doing the practice has changed my life. I've been a practicing writer for many, many years, and my life has been changed, altogether for the better, by this practice.

Now you are ready to take your own journey into the world of writing practice. Perhaps it will be a short one, just long enough for you to pick up a few useful techniques. Or perhaps, like me, you will find yourself walking this way for life.

CHAPTER 2

Starting the Journey

The journey of a thousand miles begins with one step.

—LAO TZU

As a practicing writer, you will be going on a wonderful, surprising, sometimes frustrating learning journey. This journey does not have to have a destination. Perhaps you do have some goals in mind (to write a novel or become a poet), perhaps you don't. In either case, your journey will be most satisfying if you can take it one step at a time, as if you were walking.

At first you may find this hard to do. We are all so used to speeding from place to place, so accustomed to trying to meet "I-need-it-yesterday" deadlines. We don't want to take our time; we want to *be* there already. My adult students often remind me of children on a long car trip. "Are we there yet?" the children repeat. "Am I there yet?" my adult students seem always to be asking.

"What's your rush?" I reply. "You are learning, and learning takes time. Relax. Enjoy the place you are in now before you leave it behind."

This journey of becoming a writer, or becoming a better writer, will, if you are lucky, occupy you for your entire life. Leo Tolstoy, author of *War and Peace* and *Anna Karenina,* once found a copy of one of his published books at the home of a friend. He picked it up and began reading it. After a few minutes he exclaimed, "Oh! This is terrible. *Now* I see how I should have written this." Even great writers continue to learn their craft as they walk their own paths as writers. If you've ever read any of Shakespeare's earliest poems, you will see that he learned a lot about writing between the time he wrote those and the time he wrote his later poems and plays.

Everyone has to begin somewhere with writing. Perhaps you wish that you had started earlier. Perhaps you wonder if you have any talent. The only way you are going to find out is to begin wherever you are now.

And talent, by the way, is much more common than you might suppose. I always tell my students: "Talent is the assumptions we make about other people's abilities that keep us from developing our own." Most people have the ability to write; writers can be made as well as born. The question is not: "Do I have any talent?" The question is, "Am I willing to find out whether I really want to do this?" Do you enjoy spending a lot of time by yourself? Do you have subjects you want to explore? Do you enjoy putting ideas on paper or inventing stories or making poems? These are questions you may not be able to answer right now, but as you embark on your own journey as a writer you will discover the answers.

Through writing practice, you can find out who you are as a writer: the kinds of writing you like to do, your subjects, your ideas, your own voice. I'll help you, as a guide, along your path, but it's still your path to find, your path to walk.

As with any journey, before you begin, it's helpful to know where you are starting from. So take a few minutes to write down the answers to the questions that follow; they will help you get a picture of your starting place.

1. Where are you now as a writer? (Write down anything that comes to your mind about yourself as a writer: experiences

you have had, things you like or don't like about writing, the kinds of writing you enjoy, and so on.)

2. What do you most want or need to learn about writing or about being a writer?

3. What do you think your first step as a practicing writer might be?

Some of you may have had bad experiences with writing, experiences that made you feel you can't write. Some teachers like to have you explore those as a way to recover from them. If you want to do that on your own, by all means, do. But that's not my approach. Instead, I say, "That's in the past. If you can, just let it go. Imagine that you are beginning a new journey with your writing and you are leaving all the old baggage behind."

SETTING UP A WRITING PRACTICE

One of the wonderful things about being a practicing writer is that you need very little equipment: no fancy gadgets, no special clothes, no expensive shoes. All you really need are a pen or pencil and a notebook. You don't even have to have a computer. So you can write any time you like and in just about any place you may find yourself.

Many of us, though, myself included, prefer a regular practice routine. Writer and filmmaker Woody Allen said, "I write every day. I'm very disciplined. I enjoy it...I have a perfectly sedate life. I wake up, do my treadmill, have breakfast, then I write and practice the clarinet and take a walk and come back and write again ... I do it seven days a week. I could never be productive if I didn't have a regular life."[2]

I invite you to take some time to consider how you might like to set up your writing practice. First, think about the following questions: When do you have your best energy? Do you want to write at a regular time or whenever you feel like it? Perhaps some of both?

Now imagine your ideal writing spot. Where are you? What time of day is it? What does this place look like? What sounds do you hear? What do you see or smell or touch? What are you wearing? Are you alone? With others? Is your cat curled up on your lap or your dog at your feet? Is this place silent, or is there music playing? What kind of music is it? Are there things around you that comfort and inspire you?

Now—with all these details in mind—try this simple visualization exercise:

Imagine that you are writing in your ideal place. Write, in the present tense, where you are, what you are wearing, and so on: "I am sitting on the rocks overlooking a harbor. The sun is bright and warm." If that doesn't feel right, try another picture.

Now, using the same process of collecting sensory details, repeat the visualization exercise with a place that exists in your life now, where you can actually set up a practice. Once again, imagine that you are writing in this place. Write down, in the present tense, where you are, what you are wearing, what you see or smell or hear: "I am at my kitchen table with my cat asleep at my feet. I'm wearing jeans and my oldest sweater. I've got the radio on, tuned to a classical station, but it's not loud enough to distract me. I've got a cup of coffee on the table." And so on. If that doesn't feel right, try another picture.

In looking at your two pictures, you may feel that there is an unbridgeable gap between your ideal and real writing places. Think about ways to integrate elements of your ideal place into your actual writing space. For instance, did you imagine an ideal place that has lots of light? Is there a way you could have more light at your desk?

You may want to experiment with different kinds of lighting or different chairs or different arrangements of your space to find out how you can be most comfortable. Though it may not seem like it, writing is in fact a physical activity that requires a lot of energy. You'll have more energy to do it if you are physically comfortable.

Many people adopt what I think of as the "high-adrenaline" approach to writing. They pump themselves up with coffee or alcohol or drugs and write from that particular "high." Indeed, many famous writers have taken this approach. I prefer a much more relaxed approach that enables people to maintain their health. So I encourage my students to consider things that they can do before sitting down to write (or during breaks from writing) that will help them relax and give them energy for writing. Taking a walk or a run, stretching, doing yoga or t'ai chi are among the practices that my students have found helpful. What might work for you? Think about it.

But you don't need to set up a space or find your perfect writing routine to take your first steps as a practicing writer. If you like, you can take those first steps of your journey right now. Just get yourself some paper and a pen or pencil, or sit down at your computer, make yourself as comfortable as you can—and let's play!

CHAPTER 3

Waking Up the Content Mind: The Basic Practices

Baseball fans may not realize that some fielding plays look easy only because of the preparation involved. As Hall of Fame football receiver Don Hutson once said, "For every catch I make in a game, I've made a thousand catches in practice."

—TIM MCCARVER, *Tim McCarver's Baseball for Brain Surgeons and Other Fans*

When we watch a professional baseball player stand at home plate, swing a bat, and hit a ball out of the park, we can be filled with admiration: He makes it look so easy! Professional writers, just like professional athletes or musicians, make what they do look easy (especially since we usually read their work only in its finished form). When we read a story or an essay by a skilled writer, what we see is the final fusion of content and language, just as when we watch a center fielder make a great catch we see the fusion of his ability to run to where the ball will drop and his ability to keep an eye on it.

When we watch a hitter, we can to some extent also see what he is doing. We can watch the effort in the swing; we can to some degree even feel in our own bodies some of the different muscles involved in the hitter's performance. The same thing is true when we see a musician in concert: We can watch her fingers moving across the keyboard or the violin neck.

But when do we ever get to watch professional writers engaged in actually producing pieces of writing? And, even if we could watch a writer at work, what we might notice wouldn't help us much: the click of computer keys, the slurping of coffee—these are accompaniments to the work of writing, not the work itself.

We can never actually see what goes on when a writer is at work, because all that work is happening inside her head, invisible to an outside observer. That's one of the main reasons it's so hard to learn to write. Humans learn primarily through imitation; but we can't imitate an activity if we can't watch someone doing it.

Having devoted most of my adult life to teaching writing, I've thought a great deal about what, exactly, it is that writers are doing when they are at work. I realized that, just like athletes and musicians, they are making use of particular skills. Athletes and musicians are primarily using their muscles (though, naturally, not in a mindless way). What, then, are writers using?

We're using certain parts of our minds. And, like athletes and musicians, we can improve our skills by putting ourselves into training. In this chapter, we'll explore some basic practices for training our writer's mind.

THE WRITER'S MIND: CONTENT-MIND AND CRAFT-MIND

We often think that writing is simply about words: If we could only find the right words, we tell ourselves, we could write anything. We imagine real writers, published writers, as people who sit down at the computer and effortlessly spin words out onto the screen. But while it's true that being able to use words well is an important part of writing, there's something else that's just as important: Coming up with and developing content.

When you get right down to the absolute basics, writing is pretty simple: Have something interesting to say, and say it as well as possible. Most writing instruction, though, focuses almost entirely on "how to say it" and leaves out the other essential part of writing—the "what to say." So, when many people write, all their attention is going into thinking about words, especially the mechanics of using words correctly: grammar, spelling, and punctuation. It's certainly true that skilled writers know how to use words well (and their skill encompasses far more than a knowledge of mechanics). It's equally true, though, that skilled writers have something to say, something to pass on to other people through the medium of the written word.

So, if we could look inside the mind of a skilled writer, we would see it engaged in two activities: coming up with things to say about a subject, and finding words and sentences to communicate those things to other people. We can, then, think of a writer's mind as having two main parts: content-mind and craft-mind.

What is content-mind?

That's the part of a writer's mind that comes up with ideas for things to write about and material to make use of. Skilled writers, with their well-trained content-minds, know how to grab and keep the attention of their readers through content—interesting ideas and information, scenes, stories, characters, details, and so on.

What is craft-mind?

That's the part of a writer's mind that communicates what she has to say. Craft-mind deals with two things. It deals with the "large craft"—the understanding of genre (how a novel works, for instance, or what an op-ed piece looks like), and it also deals with "small craft"—the craft of choosing words and combining them into sentences and paragraphs.

Naturally, when we are working on a piece of writing, these two "minds" often work together, at the same time. But in order to learn

How to Be a Writer

how to use each of these minds well, it's best to train them separately. (Paradoxically, though, if you undertake content practices on a regular basis, you may discover that the more you concentrate all your attention on training your content-mind, the more easily words come to you.)

If you learned to write in school, it's likely that you haven't spent much, if any, time training your content-mind. And so chances are good that, as you work on a story or a poem or a chapter of your memoir, you will find yourself stuck, blocked, unable to continue. Perhaps you will berate yourself for your lack of words. But it may not be words you lack; it's more likely that you lack material to work with. You lack content for your writing.

If your content-mind is weak, you can strengthen and develop it. Everyone has the ability to come up with content for writing, so you don't need some mysterious quality called "talent." All you need is the opportunity to practice using your content-mind without thinking about words at the same time.

In the next section of the book, we will explore the various writer's powers that give us materials for our writing. First, though, let's play with some basic practices designed to wake up our content-mind.

PRACTICE #1: FREEWRITING (REVISITED)

A writer is not so much someone who has something to say as he is someone who has found a process that will bring about new things he would not have thought of if he had not started to say them.

—William Stafford[3]

Writing is a lot like cooking. You have to gather your ingredients before you can cook a soup or bake a cake; you have to gather your materials before you can put together a story or an essay or a poem. There's an important difference between these activities, though. If you want to bake bread, you can go to the supermarket to buy the flour and eggs and sugar you need. If you want to write a story, you can't go to a store for the ingredients; you have to create them yourself.

And how do you create your "ingredients?" By using your content-mind to come up with them.

As we discussed on pages 22-28 of chapter one, freewriting is one of the best tools for finding out what's in your content-mind. If you've been freewriting regularly, you've probably noticed that often your writing will lead you to subjects you had no idea you were going to write about, or to ideas you didn't realize you had. There's something about the process of keeping the pen moving across the page (or the fingers across the keyboard) that brings things out of us that we didn't know were there. In order for this to happen, though, we have to concentrate on our thoughts and ideas, and not on our words.

Let's give this a try.

PRACTICE: Waking Up the Content-Mind

Start freewriting. (If you don't know how, see chapter one.) Remember to keep the pen (or your fingers) moving, and to let go of any critical voices in your mind.

Now, as you write, try also to let go of any concerns about language, and to put all of your attention into the material that is coming to you. Perhaps this material is details of a place, or an idea you've been playing around with, or bits of a story. It doesn't matter what kind of material you are getting; and it doesn't matter if you move from one kind of material to another.

What's important here is that you concentrate on putting down on the page whatever your content-mind has to give you right now, on the material itself, rather than on the words you are using.

After your ten minutes (more, if you like) are up, take a few minutes to notice what happened when you did this exercise. Could you feel your content-mind waking up a little bit, perhaps stretching out more than it usually does?

If you are a writer who loves language, you may resist this practice. You may feel that, for you, content and words are so inextricably linked that you simply can't stop thinking about words as you write. While I certainly respect that approach, I also want to invite you to try this practice more than once before you reject it. You may find that after a while you enjoy just letting your content-mind play without concern for words, and that the practice makes it stronger so that it serves you better.

You will also probably find that what you are saying is not very well expressed. That's inevitable, since you have let your craft-mind take a vacation while you did this practice. Since you are not producing writing for other people to read, it doesn't matter if you make mistakes in grammar or spelling, or if you can't find exactly the words you want. So, if you read over what you have written, refrain from criticizing or editing it. You don't have anything remotely resembling finished text here, so there's no point in trying to "correct" it.

THE TRUE PURPOSE OF FREEWRITING

Please remember that the purpose of this writing is not to come up with finished pieces. Although occasionally you may come up with something you are happy with and want to share with others, if you place expectations on yourself to come up with "good stuff," you will defeat the purpose of the practice.

The purpose of this practice is two-fold. First, it will help you get familiar with your content-mind and how it works. Second, if you do the practice on a regular basis, it will also strengthen your content-mind—build those particular mental muscles—so that it gets better at giving you material. The more you can practice keeping your attention on your material, rather than on language, the more easily you will be able to come up with things to say.

If doing this practice makes you feel that your content-mind is empty of interesting content, don't despair! Remember that the main purpose of this practice is to exercise your content-mind; if you do the practice, you will benefit from it, even if you don't like the stuff you produced. And after you've become familiar with the writer's powers (described in the next section), you will find it easier to come up with good material.

BASIC PRACTICE #2: COLLECTING

> *Most people who do any writing ... are handicapped by simply not knowing how to collect their material.*
>
> —RUDOLF FLESCH,
> *The Art of Readable Writing*

When you practice waking up your content-mind through freewriting, you are also practicing another key writer's skill: the ability to collect material. You're not just thinking about things you might write about, you're actually getting some of those things down on paper, in one place, so you can find them again when you want to. In the rest of this book, we'll explore many different ways to find your material; here I want to make you aware of the need to collect it.

WHY WRITERS COLLECT

Writers collect because they have to have material to work with. No one can write from nothing. One of the biggest mistakes inexperienced writers make is to attempt a draft of a piece before they have collected enough material. Before you can write successfully, on any subject, you must have lots of material to work with; it's much easier to write from abundance than from scarcity—then you can choose only the best of all your material.

In many respects, writers are no different from everyone else. They have thoughts and insights about life that shimmy through their minds at odd times; they see a man on the street wearing a red shirt and green pants; they laugh at odd bits of information that appear in a newspaper story. The difference between experienced writers and other people is that writers collect this stuff by writing it down.

I want to emphasize this point, because would-be writers seem often to think that collecting material for use in pieces of writing isn't really all that necessary. When something catches your attention, it's easy to tell yourself, "Oh, I'll remember that." But will you? Even more important, when you put that extra bit of energy into recording potential material—a thought, a word, the name of a flower, an overheard conversation—that activity helps build your content-mind.

KINDS OF COLLECTING

There are two kinds of collecting: internal collecting and external collecting. With internal collecting, you collect material from inside yourself: from your experiences, thoughts, opinions, dreams; from recollections of books you've already read or movies you've seen; from anything that's already stored in your brain. With external collecting, you collect from outside yourself: from what you notice in the world around you; from books you now choose to read, or research you do; from conversations you overhear.

You can collect at random, by jotting down ideas and observations as they occur to you, and you can also set aside some of your writing practice time to devote specifically to collecting.

In on pages 211-222 of Section Three, we'll explore the practices of internal and external collecting in detail; for now, see if you can start to get into the habit of recording any interesting thoughts or observations or pieces of information that come your way as you go about your life. Remember that being a writer is something you do, not just something you think about. Like the basic practice of putting words on the page, collecting is an essential way to be a writer because the more you collect, the more you build your content-mind. So every time you collect something, just as when you do freewriting, you can say to yourself: I am being a real writer!

THE IMPORTANCE OF KEEPING A NOTEBOOK

You can do all of your collecting in the same place where you practice freewriting, or you can keep a separate notebook for collecting. As you become a practicing writer, you will discover that more interesting ideas will occur to you, more fascinating bits of information will come your way, than you ever expected—more than you'll be able to remember. Sure, you can write those things down on little scraps of paper and stuff them into a box—some writers do—but if you want to be able to find and use this material, you're much better off with a notebook, either a real one, perhaps chosen with deliberation at your local stationery store, or a file on your computer.

If you work out regularly, you've probably noticed that as soon as you start putting on your gym clothes, your body and mind start orienting themselves to exercise. The same thing can happen when you have a special notebook to practice in (or a "Writer's Notebook" file on your computer); as soon as you sit down with it, your mind and body start to turn toward writing.

Like your freewriting, your collecting notebook must be kept private, unless you choose to share something in it. After years of schooling where doing things "wrong" usually leads to negative comments and bad grades, most adults are very self-conscious about learning anything new. So your notebook needs to be a safe place—your own private learning space—where you can experiment and play with writing.

At first you may find it difficult to make the effort to open your notebook and record your ideas or observations. As with trying to establish any new habit—exercise for instance—the first steps can be the hardest; they require overcoming inertia. Take small steps. Could you spend a minute or two writing down something you noticed on the subway instead of clicking on the television or making another phone call? Could you jot down an idea for a story instead of surfing the Net? That small step, that little bit of energy turned towards your notebook, that fulfillment of the need to put something down on the page—these apparently insignificant actions, repeated over and over, will help exercise your content-mind. And at a certain point, momentum will overcome inertia, and the practice of collecting, like that of freewriting, will become part of your life.

You may find that, as with freewriting, your critical faculty interferes with your practice of collecting: Perhaps it tells you that an idea you have will never go anywhere, or that there's no point in writing down the colors of the flowers you noticed in the park because you'll never use those details. Don't listen to it! The critical faculty tends to make snap judgments. In reality it's almost impossible to know for sure, in the moment of collecting, whether this material will be useful to you later on. Just trust your intuition: if something seems attractive or important to you, write it down. If you don't, you'll almost certainly lose it. And you never know when some detail or fragment of an idea you have casually collected will, in fact, take you someplace. To borrow an example from another field, one night Keith Richards, the guitar player for the Rolling Stones, pressed the record button on his bedside tape deck and played a bass riff that had just come into his head. Without even turning off the machine, he then fell asleep (apparently the rest of the tape recorded his snores). That riff became the now-famous foundation for the band's hit song, "Satisfaction."

Remember, though, that even if what you collect at any given time doesn't lead to a finished piece of writing, when you write things down in your notebook, you are still being a real writer. We're all so conditioned to feel that every idea we come up with, no matter how slight, must be turned into a completed piece. I urge you instead to remember the difference between practice and performance, and to spend lots of time just collecting, without any expectation of what you might do with the material you collect. Over time you will discover the subjects you want to write about and the material that is uniquely yours.

And even if you don't ever use some details you've collected, the effort isn't wasted; the act of noticing something inside yourself or in the world around you and the act of writing it down have helped you make the practice of collecting a part of your life.

You can put into your notebook anything that will fit: not only words, but postcards, articles clipped from the newspaper, snapshots, ticket stubs—anything that you, as a writer, want to keep.

KEEPING TRACK OF COLLECTED MATERIAL

Students often ask: "But don't you end up with a ton of stuff? How do you organize it?" I don't organize material that I'm collecting in my notebook as I collect it; I leave that organizing activity to another time. Periodically I will leaf through my notebook, and if some of the stuff I've collected gives me an idea for a piece of writing that I want to work on soon, I will gather all of that material into one place outside of my collecting notebook: either a file folder or a new file on my computer. I like actual (rather than virtual) folders when I am working on a piece, because when I collect another piece of information or get a brilliant idea about that piece, I can write it down on a piece of paper and simply put it in the folder. If I'm collecting information for a project that requires a lot of research, I will use several file folders and keep them all together in a big binder, or I might use a separate notebook for this particular project. If you prefer to work entirely with virtual files, it's easy to create new ones for each project and cut and paste material from your writer's notebook into the appropriate files.

With these suggestions, though, we're getting way beyond the basic practice of keeping a writer's notebook. For now, I recommend that you start small: Get yourself a notebook that you like or open a "Writer's Notebook" file on your computer. You may want to have one place in which to do your freewriting practice and another for collecting; or you may want to do both practices in the same place. If you want to decorate your notebook with drawings or pictures, or record inspiring words from your favorite writers, go for it! Your notebook is your personal writing place: Do whatever you like with it to make it your own.

PRACTICE: Collect from Your Freewriting

After you've tried freewriting a number of times with all your attention on content, you can, if you like, read through what you have written and mark anything that stands out for you. You can mark a word, a sentence, a whole passage—anything you like. If you did your freewriting on your computer, open a new document and paste into it all the bits of material you marked. If you have been using pen and paper, you can circle material or highlight it or use any other marking technique you like. You can also, if you wish, now type your marked material into the computer.

When you do this activity, you are giving yourself the chance to engage in another essential writer's practice: another level of collecting. (We'll be using this technique again in subsequent chapters.)

BASIC PRACTICE #3: READING AS A WRITER

Read, read, read. Read everything—trash, classics, good and bad, and see how they do it. Just like a carpenter who works as an apprentice and studies the master. Read!

—William Faulkner

Every writing teacher must have heard this story at one time or another: A young (or not-so-young) person wants to become a writer. "What do you read?" asks the writing teacher. "Oh, I don't read anything," says the aspiring writer. "I want my writing to be completely original. I don't want to be influenced by anyone."

Imagine a kid who wants to be a basketball player who never watches games. How would he (or she) ever learn how to play? Would-be writers who don't read will inevitably find themselves in the same position. I tell my students unequivocally: You can't become a writer, or a better writer, without reading a lot.

It's from the writers you read that you will learn the most about how to write. Long before there were creative writing programs in colleges and universities, people taught themselves how to write by reading great writers.

Unfortunately, for many people, reading means either reading for information or—thanks to English professors and literary critics—reading to "analyze" a text. That kind of reading will not help you improve your writing.

Instead, you need to learn how to read as a writer.

What that means, first and most importantly, is that you need to read for pleasure. Never mind all the books you think you should read; what do you *want* to read? I will never forget a conversation I once had with an English professor who was appalled because her thirteen-year-old son was reading *The Lord of the Rings*, which, as far as she was concerned, is trash. Setting aside the fact that at least he was reading something instead of staring at a television screen or playing video games—and many people believe Tolkien is certainly worth reading—what struck me most about her comment was the snobbish attitude it conveyed. The voices of academics and critics tend to speak the loudest to us about what books are worth reading; it can sometimes be hard for us to trust our own taste.

Read what you love: It doesn't matter what it is. If you love romance novels or nursery rhymes or science fiction, then start there. Find the writers who seem to you best at what they do; when you find a writer whose work you love, you might want to read everything he or she has written. Remember, too, that your taste can change over time, and that the house of books has many rooms, so you might occasionally want to peek into one unfamiliar to you.

When you read for pleasure, you will unconsciously absorb a writer's style and techniques. It's even more important to make this process of learning from a professional writer a more conscious and deliberate practice. You need to study the work of writers you love. So when you read, pay attention to the things that grab you. Is a character coming alive on the page? Do you like the dialogue or the way the writer explains something? Do you love her choice of words or the way her writing sounds? Notice the sentence or word or passage that makes you think, "Wow! That's great!" Then ask yourself: How did the writer do that? Read the passage a few times; read it out loud. See if you can discover what makes that piece of writing so good.

When you study a writer's technique, you are using your craft-mind. You can also build your content-mind by paying close attention to the work of writers you love.

ENGAGE IN A WRITER'S APPRENTICESHIP

As you play with the practices in this book, you will become more aware of various aspects of the work of writing. Then you can find writers who do those things well and study both their content and their technique, just as a kid who wants to play basketball like Larry Bird or Michael Jordan would study videos of how they shoot baskets. And then you can practice imitating those writers, just as would-be Larrys and Michaels try out the moves they watched on video on the neighborhood court. Many writers learn first by imitation. The writer Hunter S. Thompson, for instance, used to copy out, by hand, sentences by other writers that he liked. T.S. Eliot once wrote: "Amateurs borrow; professionals steal." Professionals steal from each other—I'd prefer to say that they learn from each other—not by using each other's exact words and ideas (that would be plagiarism, and I can think of no better way to bore oneself as a writer than to plagiarize someone else's work), but by studying the work of other "pros" to acquire new writing skills.

The poet W.H. Auden advised young writers to create apprenticeships for themselves. Becoming an apprentice was for hundreds of years the only way to learn any craft. If you wanted to become a stonemason or a baker or a painter, you would have to apprentice yourself to someone who was already licensed to practice the craft: a master. At first you would probably get menial jobs—washing the brushes in a painter's studio, perhaps. But while you were doing those things you could keep your ears and eyes open and learn as much as you could.

If you were diligent at your assigned tasks, you'd be given new ones, like mixing pigments or stretching canvases. Eventually you'd be allowed to try your hand at an actual painting, perhaps some small section of an insignificant portrait commission. If you kept learning and developing your skill, you'd be allowed to work on more complicated and demanding projects.

If you want to apprentice yourself to a writer, you can follow a similar learning path. Find a writer whose work you admire and feel you can learn from—Auden suggested choosing someone whose level of skill you sense you could achieve someday, not a writer whose way of writing feels unattainable. (He chose Thomas Hardy.) You may want to choose a writer whose books focus on subjects that interest you. Then immerse yourself in this person's work and see what you can learn. You don't need to learn everything at once; any good writer's work will repay frequent visits over time. If you do the Reflection on Your Writing practice found on page 53 regularly, you will have a sense of which element of writing you need to focus on right now, and you can study your chosen master's work—or any other writer's—with that in mind.

READ TO FILL YOUR CONTENT-MIND

Most of all, read to educate yourself, to add to your storehouse of knowledge so that you will have interesting things to share with your readers. More than any other activity, reading will build your content-mind. Follow your interests: If you love boats, read about boats; if you love food, read about food. If you want to write about a subject, you don't have to know all about it already, you can learn about it—and reading (along with hands-on experience) is the best way to learn. (For more on doing this, see *A Writer's Powers: Curiosity* on pages 114-130.)

Every good writer is an educated writer—not educated in the traditional sense of having accumulated college degrees, but knowledgeable in his or her areas of interest. It takes time to educate yourself in this way, but you'll be amply rewarded in the form of material and ideas for your writing.

Read a story or a poem or an essay (or whatever kind of writing you like) by a favorite writer. Now think about the content of this piece and jot down what comes to mind.

What kind of material has this writer used? (For instance: certain kinds of characters or events or details or ideas.) What do you like about this material? How do you think the writer got it? Why do you think she used this particular material?

BASIC PRACTICE #4: REFLECTING ON YOUR PRACTICE

> *Live the questions now. Perhaps you will then gradually ... live along some distant day into the answers.*
>
> —Rainer Maria Rilke, *Letters to a Young Poet*

It's the second class of an eight-week writing workshop. Last week we began the basic freewriting practice, and I encouraged everyone to try it at home and to purchase a notebook. Now I ask, "So what happened with your writing over the past week?" Some people did a little freewriting and had a lovely time with it. Some people didn't write at all. One woman says, "I didn't write, but I thought about writing a lot, and I told everyone at my office how excited I am about the workshop." Someone else says, "I spent a lot of time finding just the right notebook and pen; I realize my writing tools are very important to me." Another person says, "I enjoyed the freewriting, but I'm realizing I'm sick of writing about myself." Another woman said, "I realize how much I censor myself when I write. I never knew that before."

One of the wonderful things about doing writing practice is that it helps you to learn about yourself as a writer. Because this is not performance writing, because it's totally private, you have an opportunity to notice what happens inside you when you write (or when you don't). You can learn, for instance, that the practice of simply putting words on the page makes you feel very free. Or you can learn that you have very loud voices in your head that interfere with your practice: *What makes you think you could ever become a writer?* they may say, or *And what's this silly freewriting exercise you're doing, anyway?* You can learn that you prefer to write early in the morning, that you need the radio on, or that you must have silence. You can learn that you like to watch people on the subway and eavesdrop on their conversations. You can learn that you'd rather freewrite at the computer than in a notebook. You can learn that your content-mind is full of subjects you can't wait to write about. There is, quite literally, no end to what you can learn about writing and about yourself as a writer. For to be a practicing writer is, above all, to be a learner.

Cast Aside Old Perceptions

Because our educational system and, often, our parents, are obsessed with performance, many of us have been conditioned into a state where we feel we have to know right away whether we are "good" at some activity. We feel we have only two choices: excel, or forget it. It's easy to bring this conditioning to our writing practice. But if you want to become a writer, or to become a better writer, you have to be a learner, and that means giving yourself the time and the permission to learn.

To be a learner means to adopt a particular attitude towards ourselves: It means letting ourselves be beginners as writers (even if we have been writing all of our lives). Many adults have trouble being beginners; they want to know how to do things "already." But being a grown-up doesn't necessarily mean you know everything there is to know about how to write. There are undoubtedly many things about the practice and the process and the work of writing that you were never taught in school. If you let yourself abandon the I-should-know-this-already attitude and simply accept your ignorance without giving yourself a hard time about it, then you can learn whatever it is you need to learn.

Remember that you are on your own journey as a writer. What you need to learn, right now, may not be what others need. So it's very helpful to have a way to identify your own particular needs. Perhaps a conversation with a teacher or a friend will help you do this. There's also a simple writing practice that will help, while at the same time giving you another opportunity to practice putting words on the page.

REFLECT WITHOUT JUDGMENT

It's essential not to reflect on your writing practice in a judgmental way. I'm always amazed at how harsh my students can be towards themselves as writers: *I'm so bad*, they will often say, *I didn't practice at all*; or, *I practiced a little bit, but it all sucked*. I suppose, though, I shouldn't be surprised: most of us have been conditioned by our many years in school to treat ourselves as bad students who are never quite living up to the teacher's expectations. We imagine that there are always standards out there (though we probably couldn't articulate what they are), and that the only way to describe how we are doing is to measure ourselves against those standards and find ourselves wanting.

If you approach reflecting on your practice with this attitude, you will crush your spirit; and it's that spirit that gives each of us the energy to keep going in any learning endeavor. It's crucial to take note of what you have done in your practice, and appreciate—even celebrate—it, instead of focusing on what you haven't done and criticizing yourself for not doing more. When we notice and appreciate what we have done, what we have learned, then we can take that in and it becomes part of us; that's real learning—deep, not superficial. And, in becoming conscious of what we have learned, we discover, in a natural way, where we need to go next: what we need to learn, how we might learn it. And then we can take another step on our writing journey. If we notice only what we haven't done, then we never learn anything, and we stop ourselves from moving forward.

PRACTICE: Reflecting on Your Writing

Do this practice just like the freewriting exercise—that is, keep your pen moving for ten minutes, or as long as you need. As you write, turn your mind toward reflection on what's been happening with your writing over the past few weeks. What have you noticed in the content of your writing, in yourself as a writer, or both? Has anything changed for you? What's working or not working in your practice? What might your next step be? Write down whatever thoughts come to you.

As you reflect, try to stay out of the realm of judgment and let yourself simply notice and write down, without praise or blame, what has been going on for you with your writing practice. You might like to ask yourself questions like these: *What are the practices teaching me? What am I learning about writing or about myself as a writer? Where do I sense I want or need to go next with my writing? What is my writer's intuition telling me today?*

Doing this gives you the opportunity to become conscious of what you have been learning; it makes you aware of how far you have come on your journey as a practicing writer and of what you might work on next. Reflecting on your practice in this way helps you begin to listen to what I think of as your "writer's intuition"—a voice inside that knows, usually better than your conscious mind, what you need in order to develop as a writer.

BE OPEN TO LEARNING, OPEN TO GROWING

I firmly believe that it's the willingness to be a learner—to keep on being a beginner, over and over and over—that, far more than talent, will make you a writer. So strive to leave behind your judgmental attitudes, embrace your ignorance, and let yourself become aware, without shame, of what you need to learn about writing. The practice of reflecting on my learning helped me to imagine my writing self as a small child who needs encouragement and support, not criticism—or lavish praise, either—in order to grow and develop. It gave me the permission I needed to learn as a writer.

If you do this reflection practice with some regularity, you will probably find that it gives you a clearer sense of who you are as a writer and what you need next. You might notice, for instance, that doing the free-writing practice has been fun and that now you are ready to write about a particular subject that has been on your mind a lot. Or you might realize that you are getting less bothered by your spelling mistakes; you might tell yourself that someday you will work on your spelling but that for now you're not going to let the mistakes get in your way.

You can also come up with suggestions for yourself: *It's time for me to read some traditional poetry.* Or, *I can feel that I'm ready to spend some time observing people.* This practice can also be very helpful when you are working on a specific writing project. Taking some time occasionally to reflect on how it's going, to talk to yourself on the page about specific problems, can often lead you to surprising insights and solutions.

There are no right or wrong answers to these questions, or any others you might pose to yourself. This practice will help your writer's intuition become stronger and enable you to trust what it tells you. Remember that you are on your own learning journey as a writer; when you reflect on your practice you will appreciate how far you have come and discover what your next step should be.

How to Be a Writer

Perhaps some of you will find yourself resistant, at first, to the practices of *Reflecting on Your Practice* and *Reading as a Writer*. I urge you to try these practices nonetheless. If, after you've given them a fair trial, you feel they really don't work for you, then stop; perhaps you'll come back to them at another time.

On the other hand, if you find you enjoy these introductory practices, you may decide that you want to concentrate on them for a while. Go right ahead! In addition to giving you lots of practice in putting words on paper, they will help ground you in some of the essentials of being a writer and set your feet on your own writing path. Your writer's intuition will let you know when it's time to move on to the practices in the rest of this book, beginning with the next section, on developing a writer's powers.

 ## HOW TO KEEP A PRACTICE LIST

You may find that you can make the best use of your practice time if you make a list of the things you want to practice.

1. Do the Reflection on Practice exercise, asking yourself, "What do I most need or want to practice right now?"

2. Choose three or four things you want to practice and write them down on a list.

3. Post your list someplace where you can easily see it: on your computer, stapled to the front of your notebook, in your daily planner.

4. When you have a little time for writing—even as little as ten minutes—choose one of the practices from your list and do it.

5. As you learn new practices or feel the need to revisit ones you're familiar with, rewrite your list.

SECTION 2
a writer's powers

CHAPTER 4

Creativity

All writing is creative.

—RUDOLF FLESCH, *The Art of Readable Writing*

It's early on a sunny evening in Cambridge, Massachusetts. Through the open classroom windows waft chilly April air and the smells of Indian food from the restaurant next door. A dozen adults are sitting around a long table, notebooks open, pens ready. Before we start to write, though, I ask them, "What is creativity?" They give me startled looks, and then consider. Glory says, "It's coming up with something original." Heads nod around the table. John says, "It's synergistic," and Jo adds, "like mixing the same ingredients in different ways—you can take cheese and garlic and onions and tomato sauce and make pizza, or you can take the same ingredients and make spaghetti."

The idea of having to be original often scares us; but to be creative doesn't mean coming up with something no one has ever thought of before: it means coming up with something *you* have never thought or imagined or made before. Most of us have been taught that creativity is something only special people possess—those geniuses who paint frescoes on chapel ceilings or understand the structure of the atom. But there is another kind of creativity, ordinary creativity, which we all possess. That's because our brains, as scientists have discovered, are highly plastic. This means (among other things) that they are capable of lifelong learning and change, of the constant discovery of new ideas and insights, of the production of new combinations of materials.

I like this down-to-earth approach: Creativity is simply the ability to make things, not by following a ready-made recipe or a pattern, but by taking materials and combining them in one's own way. So, just as a cook needs to gather food ingredients, or a weaver needs to choose a particular kind and color of wool, so writers need materials to work with. And it's our well-trained content-minds that give us our materials: the subjects we choose to write about and the ideas, images, stories, and information that we combine to communicate what we want to say about these subjects. As you'll see in the rest of this section, we can discover our materials inside our minds, and we can also look for them in the world outside us.

Many people seem to believe that a piece of creative writing comes into being fully formed in a writer's mind, and then all he has to do is to write it down. While this may happen occasionally, it's not typical. Creativity in writing (or any other activity) is much more a process of collecting material, then selecting "bits" from that material and connecting those bits together. We can't be creative unless we have filled our content-minds with lots of material. So we need to spend a lot of time practicing the activity of collecting. In this chapter, we'll explore some practices that will help you find subjects and gather material on them. These practices will also exercise and stretch and strengthen your creative faculty, and in the process build new connections in your brain.

FIND YOUR SUBJECTS

If you enjoy freewriting—the practice of letting your creative faculty come out and play anywhere it wants to—by all means continue doing that basic practice for as long as you want to. Some of my students, particularly those who have had to do a lot of required writing, or those whose inner judges have especially loud voices, realize that, for the time being, they need to give themselves as much writing freedom as possible. The basic freewriting practice provides that kind of freedom.

Other people quickly get bored with this practice. They want more direction: They want things to write *about*.

Finding what you want to write about is a big part of being a writer. Most of the writing we have to do demands we write about subjects other people have chosen: Our professor gives us an assignment to write about the French Revolution; our boss gives us an assignment to write a report on a new product. Many professional writers, too, have assignments to fulfill. While we can learn a lot by doing assignments, we may also find them boring. Most of us find it much easier to write when we've chosen our own subjects.

If someone were to say to you, "What do you want to write about?" there's a good chance your mind would go blank. (The creative faculty, which comes up with ideas for things to write about, likes to be courted, not confronted.) You might also believe that, for your writing to be creative, you have to write only about yourself. This is not the case. Any kind of writing can be creative, on any subject.

So how can we find our subjects? Here are a few ideas.

1. ASK QUESTIONS

You can encourage your creative faculty to give you ideas for subjects by asking it questions and writing down the answers. I provide you with some questions to get you started; if you like this exercise, feel free to invent your own.

As you answer the questions, keep your pen moving. Begin with the first question and stay with it as long as you like, then move to the next one. If something that you start writing about calls to you, feel free to stay with it until your ten minutes are up. There are no right or wrong answers to these questions: Let yourself be surprised by what comes out onto the page. At the same time, if you find yourself in territory you don't want to explore, just change direction. If you prefer, you can do this exercise more than once, selecting different questions to answer each time.

- What's on your mind right now?

- What's been on your mind lately?

- What are the things you have on your mind all the time?

- The things you obsess about?

- What are you interested in?

- What do you know something about?

- What do you have strong opinions about? What are some of those opinions?

- Do you have places or people that you carry in your mind? What or who are they?

- If you could change the world, what would you do?

When you're finished, read through what you've written, and circle or underline anything that you see as a possible subject for a piece of writing.

2. Use Your Notebook

If you are keeping a writer's notebook, it will provide you with many ideas for things to write about. From time to time, read through your entries and put a checkmark beside any item or passage that makes you think: *I want to write more about THAT!*

You may find that you've been writing about a particular subject repeatedly, without realizing its importance to you.

Now make a note to yourself about the subjects that have stood out: "I see that I'm really interested in mountains." Or, "I'm writing a lot about my grandmother. I think I want to continue with this." Then write down what you sense you want to do next with these subjects.

COLLECT MATERIAL

Once you have found a subject you'd like to write about, your next step is *not* to attempt a draft. Most of us assume that is our next step: We're unconsciously following the one-step model of the writing process I talked about earlier. But if you try to go, in one step, from a subject idea to a near-finished piece, you are doomed to frustration and failure. Writing something is a *process:* It happens in stages, not all at once. You'll have a much easier time of it—and will almost inevitably produce better writing—if you begin by exploring your subject and collecting material on it. *Lots* of material.

To begin exploring your subject, imagine it as an unmapped territory that you have the task of exploring. Before you can decide what you want to say about your subject, it's *essential* to do this exploration. Most beginning writers make the mistake of trying to write a piece without taking the time beforehand to get to know their material.

Suppose you have an idea for a story about your grandmother. What materials will you use for this story? What anecdotes will go into it? What physical details? What conversations? In order to answer such questions, you need to know what material you have to work with; and you want to gather far more than you will use. Then you'll be able to choose the best materials. Before you can make those choices, though, you need to gather the material.

We explored one way of doing the collecting practice in the section on keeping a notebook in chapter three. The kind of collecting

I talked about there is spontaneous, random collecting: recording a dream or a thought or something you overheard on a bus.

We can also do collecting in a deliberate way, to help us explore a subject. As with random collecting, we can collect from inside ourselves or outside ourselves. In this chapter we'll concentrate on internal collecting. (We'll get to external collecting in chapter six: Observation.) To do this internal collecting on a particular subject, we'll make use of a variation on freewriting. Freewriting is ideal for collecting material from within because the brain stores information via associative links; the free-associative activity of freewriting helps us engage with that network of linked information. In the variation of freewriting we'll be trying next—called *focused freewriting*— we'll still make use of the free-associative process; this time, though, instead of letting our minds go anywhere they want to as we freewrite, we'll ask them to focus on one particular subject. In this way, we'll be able to collect from inside ourselves material on our subject we may not even have known was there.

PRACTICE: Using Focused Freewriting to Do Internal Collecting

Pick a subject from the ones you came up with in the Find Your Subjects exercises on page 60; write it at the top of a new page. Just as with the basic freewriting, the guidelines for focused freewriting are simple: Write without stopping for at least ten minutes, and make sure that no one sees this writing unless you choose to show it.

As you do this exercise, keep in mind that you are not writing a finished piece—you're not even writing a draft. So you don't need to have a beginning, middle, and end. You don't have to be organized. You don't have to make sense. What you are doing is *collecting* from inside yourself whatever is there right now about your subject: bits of information, stories, people, images, ideas, words, phrases, questions ... *anything!* Internal collecting is a lot like unpacking a deep storage box that you haven't opened for years. You're not making choices right now about which things you might use; you're just trying to find out what's in there. Don't censor things as they occur to you; if they seem to have something to do with your subject—however strange or tenuous that connection might appear—put them down on the page. If your mind goes blank, repeat a word or phrase over and over until you think of something else to say.

There's one important difference between the basic, "go-anywhere" freewriting and focused freewriting: The difference has to do with how much room you give your creative faculty to play in. With "go-anywhere" freewriting, your creative faculty can go anywhere at all; with focused freewriting, you give it a specific area to play in—the area of your chosen subject—and ask it to stay there. The creative faculty, as you have probably learned by now, is like an untrained puppy: It just wants to play and explore, jumping from one thing to another without any hesitation. So you may find that, like a puppy, it wants to jump outside of the "yard" you've asked it to play in. Sometimes when your creative faculty does this, it gives you a brilliant idea about something other than the subject you've asked it to play with; when this happens, you may want to jot that idea down in the margin of your notebook, or to skip a line, write down your idea, and skip another line. Then, without stopping, go right back to freewriting about your chosen subject. Sometimes, though, your creative faculty is just distracted, and it wants you to go off in some direction that has nothing to do with your subject, nor is it a good idea about another subject—it might want you to think about what you're going to have for dinner, for instance, or want you to start daydreaming. If this happens, gently guide your creative faculty back to your subject. "Yes, that's nice," you might write, as your mind starts to drift away from your subject. "I'd like to have fish for dinner. But I'm really supposed to be writing about my grandmother, so what else do I want to say about her...?" Don't be too hasty in deciding that you've gone off on a tangent, though: Often the creative faculty will draw us through many a winding lane before bringing us home to a valuable insight or piece of information. Perhaps it will turn out that your thought about "fish for dinner" leads you to a wonderful memory of your grandmother catching fish that you might otherwise not have uncovered.

Remember to keep the pen moving *no matter what* for at least ten minutes. Afterwards take a few moments to reflect on what happened with this practice: What did you notice as you did this? Was it more difficult than the basic "go-anywhere" freewriting practice? Easier?

If you like this practice, you can keep a list of things to write about someplace in your notebook where you can easily find it. Then when you sit down to practice, you can just choose a topic and do focused freewriting on it.

USING FOCUSED FREEWRITING TO DIRECT YOUR CREATIVE FACULTY

As you may have observed in the previous exercise, focused freewriting, like basic freewriting, strengthens your creative faculty, but it also has a big advantage over that "go-anywhere" freewriting approach: It gives you practice in *directing* your creative faculty.

What do I mean by "directing" your creative faculty? I mean you give it some limits to work within, a specific game to play—for example, in the focused freewriting exercise you just did, you asked your creative faculty to stay within the limits of a particular subject. Over the years I have noticed that while the creative faculty can give me wonderful surprises when I do undirected freewriting, it some-

How to Be a Writer

times seems to do its best "work" (I mean, play!) when I invite it to go in a specific direction. Contrary to popular belief, which sees creativity as equivalent to complete freedom, the creative faculty actually thrives when it is given limits.

Could you please give me some stuff about trees this morning? I might say to my creative faculty; and then, when the material about trees seems to be coming to an end, I might say, *Is there any more?* It's hard to describe this: It's not control. I'm letting my creative faculty move freely *and* I'm inviting it to explore a particular area. This way of writing with both relaxation and intention reminds me of the practice of t'ai chi. There one of the most important—and difficult—things to learn is how to infuse your doing of the t'ai chi form with a particular intention: You might be trying for relaxation in your hands and arms, for instance. But if you try to *make* that relaxation happen, it won't; if you do the form with the intention of relaxing your hands, it might. There's a fine balance here between what the Taoists call the yang principle and the yin principle: doing and not-doing. Making it happen and letting it happen. You need to let the writing practice happen, and at the same time see if you can infuse it with your particular intention for that moment.

The more you practice focused freewriting with intention, the better you will get at really concentrating when you write. We often think of concentration as something that happens only through an effort of will. But there is a kind of concentration that happens when you are very relaxed and when you have learned to infuse your writing practice with intention. You can feel it when it happens: It's like one of those flashlights you can adjust to give a thin beam of concentrated light. Athletes talk about this experience as being "in the zone"—a state where a trained batter, for instance, can perceive a baseball speeding towards him at ninety miles an hour as if it were slowly floating over the plate.

Yes, you can find your way into this state by accident, in one of those moments of grace that happens occasionally to all writers. But the only way I know to learn how to get into this state on purpose is by doing lots of practicing, with intention.

THE MANY BENEFITS OF FOCUSED FREEWRITNG

Focused freewriting, like basic freewriting, is a wonderfully adaptable tool. You can use it for anything: Writing a memo or a letter or an e-mail; planning your day; preparing for a meeting. (And if you want your meetings to be more efficient, introduce participants to focused freewriting and have everyone freewrite about the topic at hand before they discuss it; people's comments will be much more to-the-point and useful.) Start to get in the habit of thinking about things with your pen on the page or your fingers moving across the keyboard. The benefits will amaze you: You will discover things you didn't know you knew, you will get great ideas, *and* every time you use this technique, you will be exercising your creative faculty and learning how to direct it.

If you have a subject that you want to spend more time with, you can do focused freewriting on it as often as you wish. Don't be in a rush to start in on a draft; give yourself time to explore your subject. You'll be rewarded by lots and lots of material, which the practice of focused freewriting helps bring out from below the surface of your conscious mind. Once you've collected a large amount of material, then you can select the best bits to use in your draft. And if you want to take the practice of internal collecting on a subject one step further, try this: Go back to your focused freewriting and read through it slowly, in a very benign spirit—don't start editing! Instead, do two other things: Mark whatever stands out for you—a word, a phrase, an idea—anything; and write down anything new that occurs to you as you read through what you have written. When you get to the end, write down what you need to do with this material next. (Do you need to collect more material? Would you like to try putting together a draft?) What you're doing now is developing your material; you can read more about how to do this in the *Moving Toward Readers* section on pages 135-196.

It's very important to know, however, that you do not need to do anything else with this material you have collected. We're all so programmed to believe that everything we write must turn into a finished piece. Not so! When we devote ourselves to practice rather than performance, then we can explore our materials with complete freedom. We don't have to commit ourselves to any particular subject; we can flirt with as many as we like; we can have affairs with some of them and then, when we're tired of them, just leave them be. Perhaps someday we'll come back to them. Taking a piece of writing from first idea to finished draft is a lot of work; we need to feel confident that we have a subject that we want to live with for that entire process.

So I strongly encourage you to spend a lot of time exploring different subjects and collecting material on them. The more you get used to collecting through focused freewriting, the more you will train your creative faculty in preparation for the time when you find a subject you *know* you want to write about—or when you *have* to write something. You will learn that, if you know anything at all about a subject, you can feel sure that your creative faculty will help you collect your material. This practice of collecting via focused freewriting will go a long way toward building your confidence as a writer.

At the same time, the more collecting you do on various subjects that interest you, the more you build up a wonderful storehouse of material that you might use in a piece of writing someday. Your writer's notebook—and your content-mind—will become a treasure house of images, information, stories, questions, people, observations, ideas, and more.

So if you are just beginning to write, or are getting back to writing after an absence, I recommend that you do lots and lots of collecting before you try to complete a piece of writing. Fill your notebook full of all kinds of material, and then, when you are ready, you can start going through it to find the subjects that call to you most powerfully—the subjects to which you're certain you want to devote the kind of time and energy that's required to complete a writing project.

CHAPTER 5

Memory and Expertise

Speak, Memory

—Vladimir Nabokov

Many people turn to writing because they want to explore their own experiences: They want to write about things that happened to them, or tell stories they remember, or paint verbal pictures of people they have known; or they may want to use their own life stories as materials for fiction. Such writers need to find ways to bring out from inside them the material that lies within.

Some of you may feel that the things you want to write about happened so long ago that you can't remember them very well. Or perhaps you feel that you don't even *have* any experiences worth writing about. The fast-paced lives that many of us lead don't allow us much time for reminiscing. But there's a lot of useful material buried deep inside your content-mind, material that you can get access to by using your memory and searching your expertise.

In the last chapter, you tried out the practice of internal collecting. Let's now use that same practice to see what we can dig out from our memories. As you do the following exercises, you may find yourself returning to subjects you've already begun to explore, or you may open a door to a hitherto forgotten experience. Remember that you are in charge of this process; if your mind leads you someplace you prefer not to go, stop or change direction.

PRACTICE: Ask Questions

Although you might feel that you can't remember anything interesting, asking yourself questions can open the door to material you may find very useful. Try the questions below, jotting down your answers, or make up questions of your own. Start writing in answer to the first question, and then keep your pen moving as you go on to the next one. If one question sets your mind off in a particular direction, by all means continue along that path as long as you like.

- What kinds of things do you carry in your memory? If it were a knapsack, what kinds of things would you pull out?

- What kinds of places do you carry in your mind? Places you've liked? Places you'd rather forget? A city—a home—a room? A mountain—a forest—a secret imaginary place?

- What people do you carry in your mind? People you want to remember? People who haunt you? A character from a book or a movie? Some famous person you wish you could meet?

- What scenes or moments do you carry in your mind? ("The time I ... .")

- What stories do you carry in your memory? Have you known anyone who told you stories? What were they?

- What are some of your favorite memories? Your least favorite?

- If you could return to another time in your life, what would it be?

Whenever you've had enough, feel free to stop. Here's another similar exercise.

PRACTICE: "I remember ..."

Start your freewriting practice with the phrase, "I remember ... ." Write as long as you want to on one memory; then when you get stuck, write "I remember ..." again. Keep doing that until your practice time is up.

You can also write "I remember ..." and simply complete the sentence, then do that over and over, without going into detail about any one memory, until your practice time is up.

PRACTICE: Use Photographs

Take a photograph or memento that reminds you of past experiences or stories and put it in front of you while you practice. Let yourself write the story this photo or object has to tell. If you want to, give the object its own voice and let it speak to you.

PRACTICE: Collect Using Memory

Read through everything you wrote in the above exercises. Mark all the things that stand out for you. Now choose, from the items you marked, one subject you want to explore. Write that subject at the top of a new page.

Now, using the focused freewriting technique described in the last chapter, write for ten minutes about your chosen subject. Try to concentrate on collecting the details of the person or place or experience you are remembering rather than expressing your feelings about them. What time of day was it? What were people wearing? What did they do or say?

Sometimes when people do these memory practices, they worry about whether they are remembering "right." During a class, one of my students asked, "Do you have to know with absolute certainty that what you are remembering really happened the way you remember it?" And another student added, "That thought kept occurring to me, too: *But would the other people who were there remember it the way I did?*" She continued, "That thought is one of the 'edit buttons' that makes me stop writing."

Remember that all you are doing here is collecting material in your notebook; no one else will ever see it. And be aware that memory is notoriously subjective and inaccurate—the "memory police" are not going to come and get you because you haven't remembered something exactly the way it happened. During one class discussion, a woman said, "Memory is like dreams—the same quality. I was writing about how I saw the Harlem Globetrotters at Fenway Park—but I couldn't have done that, could I? And yet it's what I remember. The picture is so clear: I can *see* the chalk dust on the third base line." If you decide, eventually, to publish a memoir, you will be able to make it clear to your readers that your material is remembered experience, not verified facts.

MEMORY AS A SOURCE OF MATERIAL

If you do these memory practices over time, you will probably be surprised by what your memory and your creative faculty, working together, come up with. My students will often comment: "I had no idea all that stuff was inside me." To which I usually reply: "You can't be alive on this planet for twenty or thirty years—or more—without accumulating lots and lots of things to say."

Memory is a great source of material for writing: for poems or memoirs or essays or family histories or letters to an old friend (*Do you remember ... ?*) You can also, if you are writing fiction, donate bits and pieces from your memories to your characters and your stories; you can use your creative faculty to extract details and events from memory and then recombine them to invent people who are realistic but who never actually lived, stories that feel real but that never really happened.

At the same time, these days there seems to be a widespread belief that to be a writer one *must* excavate personal experiences and write from them exclusively. It's as if personal experience were the only source—or the truest, most valuable source—for writing, and as if memory were the only writer's power. I most emphatically do not agree with this approach.

Yes, writing about one's own experiences, and one's feelings about them, is a wonderful way to understand both, and to get to know oneself better; such writing can indeed be therapeutic. But it's certainly not the *only* way to write. And, for some people, it can even be damaging; some experiences are better left forgotten.

Aspiring writers are always being told, *Write what you know.* But what we know is not limited to our personal experience and feelings. And memory can provide us with another kind of material that's just as interesting—often, I would say, even more interesting—than the stories of our lives: namely, our expertise.

SEARCHING YOUR OWN EXPERTISE

Now that we've explored the concept of collecting subjects based on your personal memories, let's consider another natural source for great material: your areas of expertise. Here are a few exercises to play with.

PRACTICE: What Do You Know?

"What do you know something *about*?" I ask my students." Do you know how the stock market works, or about some obscure Renaissance painter? Do you know how to play the bagpipes and have lots of stories about your instrument's history? Are you a baseball fan whose mind is full of statistics about your favorite team?"

Take ten minutes to list everything you know something about. (These areas of expertise do not have to be academic or "important" subjects. Do you know something about parenting teenagers? Or about tending bar? Write those things down on your list!) Let your mind move freely, as in a freewriting practice, and don't censor what comes to you. If you get stuck, try writing, "I know ..." or "I know how to ..." and complete the sentences. Keep the pen moving.

PRACTICE: Collect Using Expertise

Look through your list and mark all the items that stand out for you. Pick one subject, and write it at the top of a new page. Now, using the technique of focused freewriting, collect onto the page everything you can think of, right now, about your chosen subject. If your mind goes blank, keep the pen moving until you think of something new.

You may find that there are gaps in your knowledge of your subject. That's good! In *A Writer's Powers: Curiosity* we'll look at how a need to know more about a subject can help you collect more material.

EXPERTISE AS A SOURCE OF MATERIAL

Any subject that you know something about can provide you with material for a piece of writing. Many writers are people who take what they know seriously enough to write about it; we call them experts in their respective fields. And expertise can inform a piece of writing in *any* genre, not just nonfiction. If you want to write stories, your characters will have to have jobs and interests (at least, one hopes so); your expertise can provide them with both. (Readers of fiction often love to learn about characters' work lives.) And you never know when a particular detail or a piece of information or an image your expertise can provide will turn out to be just the thing you need to complete a sentence or a poem.

I've noticed that most people don't value their own expertise as material for writing. Sometimes in class, after we've done this exercise, I invite each person to tell us one or two things he or she knows about or knows how to do. "I know what it's like to live in Alaska", said Leslie in one workshop. "Astrology," said someone else. "Driving a car for a living," said Elaine. "Roofing—and the ocean," said Jerrusha, adding, "When you love something, you know a lot about it." After everyone had spoken, I asked the group, "Wouldn't you want to read something about these subjects?" "Yes!" they all exclaimed.

Take the things you know about seriously; they can provide you with great material. And exploring your memory for your expertise rather than your feelings can give you a new and exciting way of using your own experiences in writing. Often students will tell me, "I'm sick of writing about myself!" Doing a lot of focused freewriting on your areas of expertise can help you turn your writing focus away from your self and out towards the world around you. The next group of practices will help even more.

How to Collect Material Using Internal Collecting

- Look through your notebook, or brainstorm a list of topics using one of your writer's powers.

- Read through your list and mark everything that stands out.

- From the topics you have marked, pick one and write that subject at the top of a new page.

- Using the technique of focused freewriting, collect everything you can come up with, right now, about your subject.

- Remember that you are not generating finished text! You are simply encouraging your content-mind to provide you with material. Later on you can decide which pieces you want to use.

- The more you practice collecting, the stronger your content-mind will become.

Memory and Expertise

CHAPTER 6

Observation

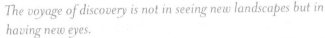

> *The voyage of discovery is not in seeing new landscapes but in having new eyes.*
>
> —Marcel Proust

We've been exploring some ways to develop the writer's faculty of memory: memory of personal experience, and memory of things we know. But there are other sources of material than what we remember; and, if we want to build our content-minds, there are other writer's powers to develop besides memory. One of the most important is our power of observation.

Most of us, these days, spend much of our lives in our heads, in a state of preoccupation and self-absorption, wrapped up in our anxieties and harangued by familiar voices that seem to run in an endless tape loop in our minds. We are obsessed with the things we have to do, or with how we can best play the starring role in what one of my students called, "the movie of my life." We rarely notice what is outside of us, right now, in the present moment. This is truly sad, for what is outside of us are riches beyond price, a writer's treasure that any of us can have for our own, if only we are willing to collect it.

Once, when humans lived in what some people condescendingly call "primitive" cultures, they *had* to pay attention to what was around them: Their very survival depended on it. They had to be

able to tell red berries that were sweet and nourishing from berries of an almost identical red that were poisonous. They had to know when a faint scuffling sound on the forest floor meant squirrels were digging for nuts and when it meant an enemy was approaching. The power of observation—of being aware of and noticing what is around us—is a natural human faculty that we are all born with. In many of us this faculty has atrophied from lack of use; but, with practice it can, in time, be regained.

HOW TO OBSERVE 1: TURN OUTWARDS

Developing your observational powers is simple: Turn your attention away from the chatter in your mind—*I wish I hadn't said that ... I wonder if I should buy chicken for dinner ... I think he likes me*—and turn it outwards, toward the world around you. Simply notice what is there: What do the clouds look like today? What is the person sitting next to you on the subway wearing? How loud is the train? How does your sandwich taste?

Though this practice is simple, you may not find it easy. For many of us, the act of engaging with the world around sends our minds instantly into the mode of evaluation and judgment. Very often we leap from attention to judgment without even realizing we are doing so: *What an ugly dress that woman is wearing!* or *I hate this music.* But observation is not judgment! Observation requires that we pay attention to what's around us not with our judging minds but with our noticing minds: *That woman's dress is red and green with yellow stripes.* Or: *This music repeats the same two sounds over and over.*

The first step in learning to observe is to slow down. These days many people (at least in big East Coast cities) live as if life were a continuing series of emergencies. *I'm so stressed!* we tell our friends, as if having too much to do and not enough time to do it were somehow heroic. It's impossible to develop your power of observation when you are rushing around all the time. So give up some of those things you think you *have* to do (so your house isn't clean, so your paper isn't in on time—will the world end?), and let yourself slow down. Then, in this state, do something simple, like sit at your kitchen table with a cup of tea or go for a walk. And simply notice what is around you: a chair, a tree, grass, sky, buildings, other people. At first you may resist this practice; it may seem so simple as to be silly. Yet observation is one of the things that good writers do; it's one of the fundamental ways of *being* a writer.

If you would like to take this practice one step further, record your observations in your writer's notebook in a practice I call external collecting.

HOW TO OBSERVE 2: DO EXTERNAL COLLECTING

One of the best ways to develop your power of observation is to use your writer's notebook to do the practice of external collecting. In this practice, you collect material, not from inside yourself, as with internal collecting, but from outside yourself. Get into the habit of turning your attention outward and see what catches your interest. When something grabs you—the odd name of a business or some words you overhear on the subway or the color of the sky at dusk— jot it down in your notebook (or someplace else, if you don't have your notebook handy; you can copy or paste it in later). Many writers keep a small notebook with them all the time so that they can capture their observations. If you write only on one side of the page, you can paste or tape the page into your large notebook later on.

This kind of external collecting is another essential writer's practice. It does two things: It trains your powers of observation, and it provides you with material you can use in your writing: ideas for things to write about, bits of dialogue, images, descriptive details, and so on. Most writers (except the terminally self-absorbed) make a habit of spending a great deal of time doing this kind of external collecting. Henry James, for instance, used to go to dinner parties in London, where he lived, and collect stories told to him by other dinner guests; later he would use some of those stories to create his novels. F. Scott Fitzgerald did the same thing; so does Ann Beattie, (who has acknowledged that after she has borrowed her friends' stories she then invites them over for dinner as a way of repaying them).

Noticing things in the world can also spark thoughts and memories. The sight of a woman with blonde hair may remind you of your high school girlfriend, while a homeless person may give you ideas for a letter to the editor about homelessness. To be stimulated into ideas for writing by the outside world is a wonderful thing. External collecting is just as valuable as internal collecting in giving you ideas for things to write about as well as material you might use someday, so I urge you to make it a regular part of your practice. You can collect at random, whenever something strikes you; and you can—and should—make external collecting a deliberate practice.

HOW TO OBSERVE 3: COLLECT SENSORY DETAILS

While observations that trigger memories or ideas are indeed useful, it's also the case that, because this kind of observation takes our attention away from the things we are observing into past experiences or thoughts, it doesn't provide the best training for our power of observation. To develop this particular power requires that we be as fully present in the world as we can—and that we use, not our intellect or our memory, but our senses. It can be difficult to stay with our senses only, and to use them to notice and to collect sensory details from the world around us. To become good at this, we need to practice. Here's one way to do that.

Take your notebook and your pen, and find a place to sit for twenty minutes or so. You can stay inside your home, if you like; it's more fun, though, if you pick another place to go: a café or a park bench or your favorite spot by a river. You might want to imagine that you are going on a collecting expedition, like a scientific explorer who goes out into the wilderness to collect exotic butterflies or plants. You won't be bringing home any specimens, though, because what you are going to do is simply to explore the world using your senses and to collect your observations in your notebook.

When you get to your chosen spot, settle yourself and start observing. Remember that we have five senses—sight, hearing, smell, taste, and touch. Try using as many of them as you safely can. If you see a tree, for instance, you may want to get close to it and run your fingers over the bark to find out what it feels like. You may want to press your nose against it to see if it has a smell. But—unless you know what you are doing—don't break off a leaf and taste it! On the other hand, if you are in a café drinking coffee, the taste of the coffee is a sensory detail you can certainly collect.

Don't worry about observing "perfectly." If this activity isn't something you do often, you may find it difficult at first. That's okay. Remember this is just practice, and be patient with yourself as you exercise and train your faculty of observation. One of the things that will happen as you practice is that you will start to learn what kind of detail each sense can provide you with. You'll learn that our eyes can give us details of color and light, shape, pattern, size, distance, motion, and visual texture. Our ears notice the qualities of sounds, such as loudness or softness, harshness or gentleness, speed, duration, rhythm, and pitch. Our fingers and skin detect texture and warmth or coolness, among other things; our nose and mouth often work together to notice such qualities as sweetness or bitterness, or heat or cold.

It's essential to remember that you are not trying to compose coherent sentences and paragraphs while you are doing this. You are just collecting. And you are collecting *only* from outside yourself. So if something you notice makes you remember a past experience, just set that aside and keep focusing on what you are taking in right now through your senses. If it helps, imagine that you are a scientist, making exact observations of the world.

Don't worry about finding the right words. Just jot down your observations in whatever words you can find. Don't write sentences, just collect details. You might write: *white table made of some shiny material; smell of cigarette smoke; blonde woman said, "He drives me crazy."* The point of this practice is to train your power of observation, so rather than seeking better words, try to observe your surroundings more closely: Rather than just writing "green leaves," for instance, get up close to a leaf and look at it. What do you observe now? Try to make your observations as specific and detailed as you can. Remember, too, that you are not judging but simply observing. If you find yourself writing something like "ugly dog" or "irritating sound" notice that the words "ugly" and "irritating" are judging words. Try to find the characteristics of the dog or the sound that have led your mind to those judgments. Does the dog have a long body and tiny legs and head, with drool coming out of its mouth? Is the sound a constant mechanical whine?

When you've done this practice for at least twenty minutes (more, if you like), stop and rest. What was it like for you to do this?

When my workshop students return from their first "collecting expedition," their faces are usually aglow with excitement, and they exclaim, "There's so much out there!" I often ask, "How many of you noticed things that you wouldn't have noticed if you hadn't been doing this practice?" Most of the time, everyone raises a hand. The world, they agree, is a rich place indeed.

Everything that you collect during this practice of external collecting is, potentially, material you might use in a piece of writing someday. You never know when a detail you gathered during one of your collecting expeditions will be just the thing you need in a poem or a story or an essay.

HOW TO OBSERVE 4: COLLECT SENSORY DETAILS FROM MEMORY

If you enjoy this practice, you can use your power of observation and your memory together, turning the practice of external collecting of sensory details into an internal collecting practice. Try this.

PRACTICE: Observe in a Memory

From your list of memories, pick one. Then put yourself, in your mind, in that place or with that person or in the middle of that event. Then use your power of observation to collect sensory details, just as you did in the previous exercise. Try to use all your senses, and, again, focus on the details themselves and not your reactions to them. Keep going back and forth between the picture in your mind and the page until you have done all the collecting you can.

HOW TO OBSERVE 5: USE SENSORY DETAILS

You may already be familiar with an oft-repeated piece of writing advice: *Show, don't tell.* Many kinds of writing, including memoir, fiction, and poetry, rely heavily on specific sensory details to create a world in a reader's mind that feels real (whether it is a real world or a fantasy world makes no difference). If we write, *Blanche was wearing an ugly dress,* that sentence will not make any pictures in our reader's mind; we have *told* the reader about the dress—passed a judgment on it—but we haven't *shown* it. How can the reader possibly know what a writer means by *ugly?* The writer must either make a verbal picture that will show the dress itself and let the reader draw her own conclusion that it is ugly, or must add to his sentences the details that show why he has made that judgment. So we might write something like: *Blanche was wearing a dress that had red and green spots on an orange background.* Or: *Blanche was wearing a very ugly dress, with red and green spots on an orange background.*

You can practice showing by going back through the details you collected on your observation expedition, or from your memory, and choosing some you like. Add any new details that occur to you. Now use these details to make a few sentences (or some images, or lines for a poem) that will make what you observed come alive in your reader's mind. Students often ask, "How many details should I use?" When you use detail in a piece of writing, how many to use—and which ones—depends on your purpose: What are you trying to make happen in your reader's mind? So as you practice the technique of showing, try experimenting with different kinds of detail—not just visual, but tactile or auditory or olfactory. See what happens when you use only a few details, or what happens when you use many. And when you read a book you like, pay attention to the places where the writing made a world (or a small piece of it) come alive in your mind. Then try to figure out what the writer did to make that happen. Then practice that technique yourself. The more you study and practice, the more you will be able to "show" on the page anytime you want to.

UNDERSTANDING OTHER KINDS OF SPECIFICS

One of the things that will happen if you practice exercising your power of observation is that you will notice that everything in the world is an individual. At first glance the leaves on a maple tree may look exactly alike; but if you inspect them more carefully, you will discover that they are not: one will have a tiny hole eaten out of it by a caterpillar; another will have a white spot of bird dropping on it; yet a another will be slightly bigger than the other two. Even among machine-made things there can be differences, especially once they have been handled by people and made a part of their lives: We personalize our cars, our clothes, our apartments.

Recognition of the particularity of things in the world is essential for writers, because good writing is always grounded in *specifics*, not generalities. While it's true that we often talk to each other in generalities—*We had a good time; The food was delicious*—we can't communicate much that way. Generalities are vague, sometimes nearly meaningless: *Have a nice day.* For our speech, or our writing, to communicate we need specifics: specific pieces of information, specific examples, specific details.

If you are trying to convince someone that the 2009 Red Sox were still a better team than the Yankees, even though the Yankees landed Mark Teixeira, you need specifics to do that. If you saw a film and are telling your best friend how great it was, you need specifics to do that. If you are telling a story or revealing a person's character, you need specifics to do those things, too. Specifics don't have to come only from observation; they can come from memory or imagination or our reading or anyplace else we collect from. But the regular practice of observation can teach you a lot about the difference between a generality—a tree, for instance—and a specific— the dying silver maple tree in front of the library.

You can also train yourself in being more specific through the following exercise.

PRACTICE: Be Specific

Write as many general statements as you can: *That was a great movie!* Or *We had fun at the party.* Try for at least ten. Read some of these aloud, imagining that you are someone else. What do you notice? Most likely, as your imagined listener, you will find yourself wondering, *What does that statement mean?* General statements are usually empty statements; when we think about them, we don't know what the writer is trying to say.

Now take each one of those statements and make it more specific, inventing whatever details seem appropriate. *That was a great movie! It had two car chases and three murders.* (Is this what *you* would call a great movie? Making a general statement more specific helps readers understand what the writer is saying, which often is different from what the general statement might mean to them.)

Now read some of these out loud, first the general statement, then the specific. Can you hear the difference?

Any kind of writing, no matter what kind—creative writing, business writing, academic writing—needs to be grounded in specifics. In casual conversation, especially with people who know us, we can get away with general statements; the meaning of our words is enhanced by our tone of voice and body language. But in writing, all we have is what we say. If you are trying to persuade people or make an argument or present an opinion, you can't make only general statements—they will slide through your reader's mind without impact. Give examples, give statistics, give anecdotes—give whatever you can to *show* your reader what you mean.

HOW TO OBSERVE 6: USE FOCUSED FREEWRITING

It can take a lot of practice to get comfortable using sensory details and other kinds of specifics in our writing. So, if you like, pick a subject to do some focused freewriting on, and then, as you write, try to put some of your attention into being specific. At first you may find this very difficult; it may spur your critical faculty into action: *That's not a specific!* If you find yourself becoming impatient or frustrated, leave this practice until later on. If you can, though, just keep your pen moving as you try to get more specific: You can write down a word or a phrase, then have the thought, *Oh, that's not specific enough!* and then come up with a more specific way of saying the same thing. Don't try to create elegant writing! The point of this practice is to accustom you to writing while focusing your attention both on one particular subject *and* on being specific (a bit like trying to walk and chew gum at the same time). This practice will help you get into the habit of bringing specifics and sensory details into your writing.

While we do need generalizations occasionally when we write, relying on them exclusively will not only bore our readers, it will make us mentally lazy. The practice I've just described will not only improve your writing—specifics make things *happen* inside your readers—it will also wake up your mind!

HOW TO OBSERVE 7: USE OBSERVATION AS A SPRINGBOARD

Here's another way to use the details you collect through the practice of observation.

PRACTICE: Freewriting with Sensory Details

Collect some sensory details from the world around you or from your memory—or just look through your notebook for some you have already gathered. Mark the ones that stand out for you, and add any more that occur to you now. Then, by doing some freewriting—focused or "unfocused," as you wish—let your creative faculty play with these details and see what happens. Use the details as a springboard to take you further into a memory or into an imagined world or into some reflection ... or anywhere you like.

THE REWARDS OF OBSERVATION

Get into the habit of engaging in the practices of observation and external collecting and you will rapidly strengthen your observational skills. And the more you observe, the more you fill your content-mind with material that will be of use to you in your writing.

Beyond its ability to give you material, though, the practice of observation has other value: It can change your life. By simply being present and just noticing, without judgment, what is around you, you may find yourself becoming more calm, more grounded and centered in your life. The more you pay attention to the richness of the world, the more you allow your interest to be absorbed by things outside of you, the more interesting a person you will become. And the more you pay attention to the world outside you, the more it gives back: by a kind of miracle, it will become a more interesting place. Things that you previously never noticed at all, or only half-registered, will astonish you daily: the way the sun slants on the wooden kitchen table in the late afternoon; the sound of a friend's voice; the taste of chocolate ice cream. Like a child, you may come to live, at least some of the time, in a state of wonderment.

The poet William Blake once urged us "to see a World in a Grain of Sand and a Heaven in a Wild Flower."[4] If you devote yourself to the practice of observation, your path may very well lead you to a place where you can do that, to the enrichment of both your writing and your daily life.

HOW TO OBSERVE: THE BASICS

- Slow down. Take some relaxing, deep breaths. With each exhalation, try to let go of some of the mental chatter cluttering your mind.

- Now turn your attention outward, away from the thoughts in your head, and toward one thing or person or animal in the world around you.

- Using one sense at a time, see what details you can collect about what you have chosen to observe.

- As you observe, try to simply notice sensory details, like colors and sounds, without passing judgment.

- Don't worry about finding exactly the right words for these details. Concentrate on the act of observing. Instead of searching for words, try to observe more closely.

- If you like, collect some or all of these details into your notebook.

CHAPTER 7

Imagination

... imagine what you are writing about. See it and live it. Do not think it up laboriously, as if you were working out mental arithmetic. Just look at it, touch it, smell it, listen to it, turn yourself into it. When you do this, the words look after them-selves, like magic.

—TED HUGHES, *Poetry in the Making*

Pick out a few details from your observations, or read over one of the sentences you made from the details. Close your eyes and remember the words; let them make a picture in your mind. That picture is called a mental image; and in making it you have used another of the essential writer's powers: the imagination.

WHAT IS THE IMAGINATION?

The imagination is a natural human faculty, one we are born with; and *everyone* has one. Then why do so many adults think of themselves as "unimaginative?" Primarily because most people—including educators, who should know better—don't really under-stand what the imagination is; they think it's merely the ability to make things up or to create fantasy. The imagination can do those things, but that is definitely not its most important function.

If the imagination is not fantasy, if it is not invention, then what is it?

The imagination is the mental faculty that lets us create in our minds pictures of things that are not actually present to our senses.

To understand this better, you might like to try a simple exercise: Close your eyes, and then bring to your mind a picture of what you ate for breakfast. Try to make the picture as detailed as possible: Let yourself not only see, but smell and taste and feel—even hear— the cereal or the toast and coffee. Once you've got this picture in your mind to your satisfaction, open your eyes and look around you. Is your breakfast actually there before you, present to your senses? Unless you are reading this lesson while you eat breakfast, the answer will be no.

Now consider, for a moment, how amazing it is that our imaginations can do this—can create a mental picture of something that isn't in front of us. If observation is like sketching from life, imagining is like painting in the studio, without a model. I believe that the imagination is one of the marvels of the human brain; perhaps it is the faculty responsible for our having become human. Certainly without it humans could never have developed culture and art and music and literature.

Many people, by the way, assume that memory and imagination are the same thing. They are not. They are certainly linked, but they are not the same faculty. Memory enables us to retain pieces of information —*two plus two equals four*, for instance, or *Saskatoon is the capital of Saskatchewan*—but we don't necessarily imagine anything in connection with those pieces of information: When we hear them or read them or say them, we don't get any mental pictures. Similarly, we can remember that something happened, or that we did something—we can even report those events—without our imagination being involved at all. Try telling a friend in casual conversation

How to Be a Writer

what you did last week; chances are good that neither you nor your friend will get any mental pictures.

THE NEGLECTED IMAGINATION

Perhaps you weren't able to imagine your breakfast as vividly as you wanted to; perhaps it was difficult for you to do it at all. Does that mean that somehow you don't have an imagination? No, it doesn't. *Everyone* has an imagination; without one, we couldn't function. Human brains are designed to make sense of the world through sensory images. From birth, we are constantly absorbing information about the world around us through our senses, and turning that information into mental images. If we want to, we can also let our creative faculty and our imagination work together to create new images. We all use our image-making ability quite unconsciously when we dream. Where we may differ is in our ability to make conscious use of those images, to call them up in our minds when we want to. Why is that?

There are several simple answers to this question. First, many of us rarely take the time to use and exercise our imaginations. Consider what happens to other parts of our bodies when we don't use them. If, for instance, you don't use your arm for years, eventually the muscles and ligaments will atrophy. Then, when you try to do something with that arm, you won't be able to. This is the situation that most of us are in with our imaginations: It's not that we don't possess a faculty of imagination, it's that, for most of our lives, we haven't had a chance to *use* it.

Partly that's because many of us, as I said in the section on observation, tend to live our lives in our heads, oblivious to the world around us. Our brains are not registering sensory images because we're not paying attention to them. Instead, we're focusing on our thoughts and opinions; we're engaging in "self-talk" rather than letting our minds absorb sensory information.

A second reason many people feel they have no imagination is that their lives are crammed with activity. Once, in a workshop session when we were discussing the imagination, several people said, "Our lives are so fast-paced now that we don't have the time to imagine." To work well, the imagination needs to be in a relaxed state. When you are rushing around and under stress, it's just about impossible for your imagination to operate as it was designed to do. Perhaps it's no wonder, then, that another one of my students once commented, "We use our imaginations to *worry*."

Here's a third reason our imaginations may not be as strong as we'd like them to be: We usually don't get much chance to exercise and develop our imaginations at work. In the highly complex technological cultures of the twenty-first century, survival depends not on one's ability to make mental pictures, but on one's intellect. To sit at a computer processing some kind of "data" all day, one need not use one's senses or one's imagination (in fact, paying attention to one's senses is probably a liability), one needs instead to concentrate on manipulating pieces of information that have been essentially divorced—or abstracted— from sensory reality. If, for instance, your job is to schedule UPS pickups of packages for your company, you will be entering that information into your computer without ever seeing what one of the packages looks like or feeling its weight, and so it's unlikely that you can make a mental picture of it. I would guess that most people in highly industrialized countries spend at least some of their time in manipulating such abstract information.

In her wonderful book, *Animals in Translation*, animal expert Temple Grandin tells a story of a U.S. government program in the 1960s that effectively eliminated a deadly worm that attacks livestock. She goes on to comment that it would be very hard these days to get such a program going because "today government regulatory agencies are all run by people who have been to college, but who in some cases have never even been *inside* a meat-packing plant, let alone worked in one."[5] These bureaucrats, she says, are caught up in abstract thinking about animals, rather than knowing them through their senses. Grandin goes even further: She says that most people these days are in this position, they are too "abstractified." What she means by this is that most people are caught up in their *ideas* about the world around them, rather than knowing the real world directly.

Grandin's description of USDA officials who create regulations for the livestock industry based on their ideas about animals rather than actual hands-on knowledge made me laugh when I read it because it's such a perfect description of most academics. In traditional higher education, the entire focus is on abstraction, on training the intellect: on developing *ideas* about reality rather than engaging directly with the world, using our senses and our imaginations.

And here we arrive at the main reason most of us don't have a strong, well-trained imagination: Except, perhaps, in early childhood, the academic system that most of us had to go through does not value the imagination; we don't get any training in using and developing it. Instead we are forced to devote our energy and attention to the rote memorization of facts and concepts, and to the development of only one mental faculty—the intellect.

Some people are lucky: They keep using their imaginations despite school—they're often the ones, I suspect, who get bad grades but go on to become famous artists or writers or musicians. But most of us, trying to be good students, are forced to sacrifice our imaginations to the tyranny of the intellect. The result is that we may be able to think and argue clearly, and to write down our thoughts and arguments (useful, though limited, skills), but we cannot create writing that comes from our imaginations and that speaks to the imaginations of others. That's not because we have no imagination, or no talent; it's because our imaginations have not been trained and educated—they have been neglected and allowed to atrophy. After over two decades of teaching writing, I am convinced that most of my adult students are held back in developing their abilities as creative writers primarily because they are victims of an academic system that entirely ignores the imagination. Rather than being full of images, their content-minds are crammed with ideas.

HOW MASS MEDIA AFFECT YOUR IMAGINATION

There's one more reason why many of us can't use our imaginations in writing the way we want to: We live in a culture that bombards us constantly with deliberately constructed artificial images: advertisements on billboards and in magazines; the fast-moving images of television and movies. I would guess that never before in human history have people been subjected to such a constant barrage of manufactured images (unless, perhaps, under some form of torture). Many recent studies have demonstrated the negative effects of watching television, showing that this activity impedes children's abilities to read, write, think, socialize, and engage in physical activity.[6]

The effect of movies and television on their imaginations—and on our own—is no less dire: Our imagination, a faculty that is designed to be active, to *make* images, is being provided constantly—for those who watch television and go to lots of movies—with images that are already made. The result, I believe, is that many people's imaginations have become too weak to serve them when they want to write. As writers we are, I think, particularly vulnerable to the negative effects of television; it can, without our realizing it, determine the content of our writing, and it can undermine our confidence by making us feel, as some of my students have noted, that there's no way we can write anything as powerful as what's on television.

Close to fifty years ago, a psychologist named Richard de Mille wrote: "The average unimaginative high school graduate is reported to have completed 10,800 hours of schooling—and to have watched 15,000 hours of television.[7] Only sleeping has taken up more of his time. A great many of those hours, especially during the preschool and early school years, have been spent watching animated cartoons and live action fantasies." Today the situation is even worse: Children and adults alike are confronted with a constant stream of manufactured electronic images, not only from television and movies, but also from video games and computers. A recent study, revealed that "most children between 2 and 18 years old are exposed to an average of 6 ½ hours of daily media exposure, of which television is the most dominant." (Radio and audiotapes, unlike television, do encourage the active use of the imagination: just listen to Garrison Keillor's monologues on *A Prairie Home Companion*, or, if you like baseball, try listening to a radio broadcast of a game.)

Today's studies confirm what de Mille had to say half a century ago about the effect of ready-made images on our imaginations: "Television and comic-book fantasy can hardly be expected to cultivate the imagination, because [that fantasy] is already completely formed, on the screen or on the page. Nothing is left for the child to do but absorb it. The experience of the child is passive. It is not *his* imagination that is being exercised, but that of some middle-aged writer in Hollywood, New York, or Chicago."

As with any other faculty, if you want to be able to use your imagination at will, you've *got* to exercise it. And to do that, I believe that first you have to set it free. So I encourage you to liberate yourself from as much of the onslaught of images from the mass media as you can. Curtail your television watching. Limit your movie going. Give up the glossy magazines, or limit the number you read. Set your Internet browser to block images.

Setting your mind free from mass media images will give you time to use your own imagination. Instead of coming home from work and turning on the television, try relaxing and resting a bit, and then give yourself time to do some imagination practices. I suspect you will be surprised and delighted by the results.

RECLAIMING YOUR IMAGINATION

Even if you have not consciously used your imagination for years, you can still reclaim it. And if you want to do creative writing, you will need to have a strong imagination to rely on. That's because, while the content of academic and professional writing comes from the intellect, the content of stories and poems and scripts comes from the imagination. The content of academic and professional writing is information and ideas and opinion; the content of creative writing is primarily pictures, or *images*. That doesn't mean that a piece of creative writing is devoid of ideas; it means that those ideas are not stated directly through argument, as in a piece of expository writing—rather, they are embodied in images. A skilled piece of creative writing is always more powerful than a piece of expository writing because it speaks both to the imaginations of readers and to their intellects; academic and professional writing speaks only to the intellect.

The academic system teaches us to think abstractly. But the imagination provides us with another way of thinking that is just as valuable: thinking in pictures. Skilled creative writers know how to make pictures in their own minds, and they also know how to use language to communicate those pictures to their readers. Skilled creative writers, to put this another way, have content-minds that are filled, not with ideas, but with images. (Creative people in science as well as the arts make use of well-trained imaginations in their work; you may find that, once you start exercising your imagination, it will help you at your job as well as with your writing.)

If, like most adults in this culture, you are used to making writing only out of information and ideas, you may feel a little strange at first trying to work with images. I urge you to remember that you are a beginner in this realm of the imagination, and to let yourself play, without judging the results.

If you want to reclaim your imagination, you may need to find ways to be less "in your head"—less caught up in thinking, and in thinking about thinking. One of the best ways to do this is also the best way to feed your imagination with healthy images: Turn your attention outward, away from your thoughts and reactions and judgments and simply notice what is in the world around you. A powerful imagination depends on a well-exercised faculty of observation.

EXERCISING YOUR IMAGINATION

A well-trained imagination is essential for any kind of writing that we call "creative," writing that speaks to the imaginations of readers and feels "real" to them. In the last chapter we discussed the advice writing teachers often give: *Show, don't tell*. What they mean, I think, is: *Make pictures for your readers*. Usually in writing workshops the technique of showing is taught by focusing on word choice. While choosing the right words is certainly important, it's also true that we can't create vivid pictures in words unless we can first make those pictures in our own imagination. If we want to make something come alive in our reader's imagination, we must first have given it time to come alive in our own. So, following the learning principle of practicing skills separately, I urge you to spend lots of time exercising your imagination, separately from actually using it to write.

Let's begin with some basic practices for creating mental images. I doubt that any of these exercises will upset you, but if anything happens that makes you uncomfortable while you're doing them, by all means stop. You'll need to close your eyes to do these exercises, so read over the directions for each one a couple of times before you begin. Or you may find it helpful to have a friend read you the directions while you do each exercise. In either case, you need not worry about getting the details of the images exactly right.

PRACTICE: Use Your Visual Imagination

Close your eyes. In your mind imagine a blank sheet of white paper. Now imagine the outline of a square, drawn in black lines, on that paper. Don't worry if it isn't exactly square.

Now fill the square with red. Got that? Now change the color to green. Now make it yellow instead.

Keep the yellow color, and turn the square into a circle. Make the circle blue. Now make it blue and yellow, in any pattern you like.

Now keep that pattern, and turn the shape back into a square. Then turn the square blank again, erase the page, let go of the image of the page, and open your eyes.

How did that go? What happened?

If you were able to do this exercise, you used your power of imagination—you pictured something that is not actually present in front of your eyes. You may have found it easier to picture some colors than others; that's fine—you don't have to do this perfectly. And if you had difficulty, don't despair; with regular and frequent practice you can easily recover your ability to imagine.

Although we tend to think of images as only visual, in fact every sense has its own kind of imagination. People who are great cooks can imagine the taste of ingredients; musicians can imagine sounds. You can develop these aspects of your imagination as well, with practice.

Sounds

In your imagination, create silence. Now imagine the sound of a car engine. Change that sound to the sound of a dog barking or howling. Let that sound go, and imagine the sound of flowing water. Let that sound go, and imagine the sound of someone singing. Return to silence. Open your eyes.

What was it like to do this?

Touch

Now imagine that you are touching a flower petal. Feel it under your fingertips. Notice how it feels. Let that image go, and bring in an image of touching something made out of thick wool. Now let that one go, and bring in an image of touching something cold, like ice cubes. Let the ice cubes melt, warm the water if you like, and bring to your imagination the sensation of water on your skin. Notice how that feels. Let that image go, and imagine touching something made of wood. Let that image go. Open your eyes.

What was it like to do that? What happened?

Smell

Close your eyes. Imagine the smell of soap. Change that image to the smell of wood smoke, then to the smell of auto exhaust. Now try imagining the smell of a flower you love, and then the smell of your favorite food.

What did you notice as you did this?

Taste

Imagine the taste (including texture) of scrambled eggs. Almonds. Chocolate. Coffee or tea. Your favorite food.

You will probably find that your imagination is stronger with some senses than with others. You can strengthen the weak ones, if you want to. When you are observing—or living your life—pay attention to what your senses are telling you. Practice looking at something and really seeing it. Look more closely. Then close your eyes and see what you can re-create in your imagination. Keep going back and forth from observation to imagination until you're happy with the image in your mind. Do this practice with your other senses as well.

PRACTICE: *Imagine Without Words*

You'll have noticed that you don't need words to practice using your imagination. In fact, when you do these imagination practices, it's best to focus your attention on making the images and not on finding words for them. Later on in your practice you may want to spend some time trying to put your mental images into words. For now, just concentrate on using and strengthening your imagination.

You can practice using your imagination anytime you like. Just relax with your eyes closed and let your imagination make pictures. They can come from anywhere you like: from personal experience, from observation, from reading. Remember that you are in control of your practice: If images come into your mind that you don't like, just wave them away. Try starting with a simple image—say, your neighbor's cat. Get the picture in your mind and then explore it using various senses. Don't search for words; just let your imagination make the image with more and more details. Can you see the way the sunlight illuminates individual hairs in the cat's fur? Are they different colors? Imagine petting it. How does that feel? Can you hear the sound it makes when it purrs?

If you like, after you've practiced for a while with simple images, take one and let your imagination paint in more details—other figures, perhaps, or a background. See how much detail you can hold in your imagination at once. Once you feel comfortable with static images, try letting the pictures in your mind move in some way. (Can you imagine that cat being chased by a dog?)

The more you practice using your imagination in these ways, the stronger it will get, and the more confident you will become in its ability to create images for you anytime you want. And there is an added benefit to these imagination practices where we don't try to find words for our images: They seem to be amazingly useful at creating a state of mental calm and relaxation.

PRACTICE: Collect and Make Pictures

Once you've gotten comfortable with using your imagination, you can add the practice of collecting—writing down in your notebook—what it gives you.

Look back through your observations or through the material you've collected from memory, and pick something you'd like to use to exercise your imagination. Keep it simple, for now. A single place, person, or moment—not a whole experience.

Now, using your imagination, put yourself there with that person, or in the place or moment. Using as many senses as you can, re-create that person or place or moment in your imagination. Now jot down as many sensory details as you can, remembering the importance of *specific* details, just as you did when you were outside doing external collecting. Keep going back and forth between using your imagination and taking notes. Concentrate on exercising and stretching your imagination to give you clearer images rather than on the words you use.

Here you are collecting sensory details, just as you did with the observation practice; but instead of collecting from the world around you, you are collecting from your imagination (in collaboration with your memory or your faculty of observation).

Now look back through your list and select some details you can use to get that picture in your imagination onto the page in words. If you can't seem to find the language you need, see if you can make the picture in your mind clearer rather than straining after the exact word.

How did that go? Notice the process you used: First you made the picture in your mind; then you collected as many details as you could; then, from your collection, you selected certain ones to make your picture.

You may want to try this exercise again, this time picturing a person (or animal or object) in motion. Collect the sensory details, then select the ones you want to use to make your verbal picture.

PRACTICE: *Make Pictures for Readers*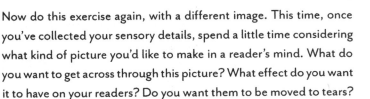

Now do this exercise again, with a different image. This time, once you've collected your sensory details, spend a little time considering what kind of picture you'd like to make in a reader's mind. What do you want to get across through this picture? What effect do you want it to have on your readers? Do you want them to be moved to tears? Delighted? Scared?

While it's absolutely fine to practice making mental pictures without thinking about a reader, when you come to write something that is designed for the eyes of others, you need to consider the effect you want your word-pictures to have on them. We always have to make choices about what to include and what to leave out, and specific details need to be chosen because they will make something particular happen in your reader's mind. We can't just throw details at random into our writing the way we might toss raisins into our breakfast cereal; we have to choose them to serve our purpose. It can be difficult, at least at the beginning, to come up with specific details and choose among them at the same time; so you may find it helpful, even when you are working on a piece you hope to complete, to follow the process of collecting the details first, then selecting the ones you want.

Once you've selected details, use them to write a short passage that will create in your reader's mind the effect you desire.

Now, if you can, find someone you trust to whom you can read what you wrote. Explain that you are doing a writing practice so you don't want any evaluation of what you have written; you simply want to know what happens in his or her mind upon hearing these words. Read out loud what you wrote in this exercise, and ask your reader, "What effect does this have on you?" Then ask, "Which words or sentences made pictures in your imagination?" (For more details on using other people to help you write, see Section 3: *Moving Toward Readers* on pages 135-196.)

If you practice trying out your experiments in showing on other people, you'll soon learn whether your words are creating the effects you want them to have.

PRACTICE: Read for Pictures

In school we're taught to read for information. We're taught to analyze what we read. We are not taught to use our imaginations. But when the Russian writer Vladimir Nabokov taught literature at Cornell, he taught as a writer, not an academic; and so, when he had to give final exams, he would ask his students to answer questions like, "What color were the seats in the train in *Anna Karenina*?" He wanted his students to let the words of the writers engage their imaginations. As a practicing writer, he knew that then they would truly know the books in ways that they never could through mere analysis.

It's a crime that almost no one teaches literature in this sensible way. Fortunately, it's easy to do it on your own; you most likely read this way already.

Here's the practice: Read something and take the time to let the words work on your imagination. See if they make sensory pictures in your mind. Then, when you find a passage that does create powerful pictures, try to figure out how the writer did that. What kinds of sensory details did he or she use? In what order? Perhaps you want to try writing an imitation of the passage. (You can also, if you like, exercise your imagination by listening to audiotapes or CDs of stories or poems or plays.)

 ## HOW TO IMAGINE: THE BASICS

1. Relax your body. Take some slow, deep breaths. Relax your mind and, as you breathe, let your thoughts go.

2. Look through the material you have collected in your notebook using your writer's powers. Make a list of some things you'd like to imagine. Start small, with one character or place or thing. Later on, you can practice imagining entire scenes.

3. Examine your list, marking the items that stand out for you. Pick one, and write it at the top of a new page.

4. Now close your eyes and imagine your subject. Use all your senses, as appropriate, to bring your subject alive in your mind. Try to make the images as detailed as possible, and remember that you can, if you wish, draw details from many different sources, including just plain making them up.

How to Be a Writer

5. Begin with a static image—what a person looks like, for instance—then, if you like, continue with some movement. What is your character doing? Can you hear her voice? What is she saying?

6. If you wish, try writing down the details your imagination has given you. If you get stuck, don't strain for words. Instead, close your eyes and make the pictures again.

IMAGINATION AND CREATIVITY: MAKING NEW IMAGES

Perhaps by now you are wondering: *But doesn't the imagination do more than just give me images? Doesn't it make things up?*

Yes, it does. But how?

Imagine a Japanese cherry tree in bloom. Imagine the smell of the tundra in the Arctic. Imagine the feel of rock at the bottom of the ocean. Imagine a pluseac, or a grinx.

Chances are, unless you've actually been to the places where you can experience these things, or seen pictures of them in a book or on television (and if you're familiar with a pluseac or a grinx, please let me know!), you won't be able to make images of them ... unless you make them up. And to do that, you call on images you already have and combine them in new ways. You might think of this process as your imagination and your creative faculty working together. To experience how this can work, try the following practices.

PRACTICE: Invent

1) Imagine a place you'd like to be in. Not a place you've actually visited but a place you construct with your imagination. Use

this faculty to imagine the sensory details of this place. Jot them down; keep going back and forth between your imagination and the page. Then select the details you want, and write a description of the place.

This is an example of collaboration between your creative faculty and your imagination. You're drawing on images you have stored and combining them in new ways: perhaps you imagined trees with purple leaves—you couldn't have done that if your imagination weren't already familiar with images of a tree, a leaf, and the color purple.

2) Imagine a dog. Imagine the dog eating a bone. Crossing a street. What does the street look like? What sounds are there? Now imagine that the dog is running. Imagine that it is running down the street, weaving among pedestrians, leaping over cars. Now it's leaping over a bus! Now a house! Now a ten-storey building!

Did you find it difficult to do this? Most likely you didn't: Your creativity and imagination probably worked together effortlessly to make these pictures. The combined power of our imagination and our creativity can bring into being, first in our minds, then, if we like, on the page, something that has never before existed. Try this practice again with a person or animal or object of your choice, and with movement of your choice: Can you see in your mind the way a person's lips move into a smile? Can you hear the sound of the getaway car leaving the scene of the robbery?

3) Pick a person or a place or an object, real or invented. Use your imagination to picture him or her or it, and collect the details it provides you with. Then use your imagination to put yourself *inside* that person (or place or thing) and let it speak. What

does it notice in the world around it? What does it see or hear or touch? What else does it have to say?

4) Picture two people having a conversation. Practice making auditory images by hearing in your imagination what they say to each other. If you like, write down their words.

If you enjoy these practices where imagination and creativity work together, make up your own.

The writing that results from this collaboration of the imagination and the creative faculty is what we call "creative writing"—the genres of fiction, nonfiction, poetry, playwriting, screenwriting, and so on. For each of these genres there are probably hundreds of "how-to" books available, and at some point on your writing journey you may want to consult some of them. Along the way, though, I recommend that you also do lots of practice in letting your creative faculty and imagination collaborate: Invent people and places, tell made-up stories.

I suspect that the intercourse that takes place between the imagination and the creative faculty is something we do best not to examine too closely. The process by which experiences and images and questions and details combine in our minds to make something new is a profound and mysterious one. Better, I think, to just let ourselves play—invent our own writing games—and see what we can learn from them.

It's also helpful if we can learn to let go when we allow these two faculties to play together; for there is an essential part of writing that is "not writing." And to learn how to "not write," we need to be aware of, and to develop, another writer's faculty: the subconscious.

CHAPTER 8

The Subconscious

> *Your subconscious mind does more writing than you think.*
> —WILLIAM ZINSSER, *On Writing Well*

One of the most important parts of writing is not writing—*if* you know how to do that.

"Not write?" you may respond. "Hey, I already know how to do that! When it comes to writing, I'm the world's greatest procrastinator!" But do you know how to make use of your tendency to procrastinate? Do you know how to make good use of the time when you are not writing?

There appears to be a kind of on-off rhythm to everything in nature: day and night; waking and sleeping; inhalation and exhalation; activity and rest. In t'ai chi the components of this rhythm are called *yang,* the active principle, and *yin,* the receptive principle. A crucial part of the practice of t'ai chi involves experiencing and expressing the alternation of yang energy and yin energy, learning both how to do and how to "not-do." The practice of writing can be enhanced in an extraordinary way when we learn how to use both of these energies, the yin as well as the yang.

But how do we do that? First, we need to become aware of the difference between the state of activity and the state of receptivity. That can be very difficult. In present-day Western (espe-

cially American urban) culture, the basic on-off (active/receptive) rhythms of nature, which sustained humans for millennia, have been replaced by the constant "on" state of a machine—especially electronic machines like computers. Like such machines, many of us live our lives in a state of being almost constantly "on": We rev ourselves up with various stimulants to do all the work demanded of us; and then when we're not working, we're out doing something "fun." All our lives—except when we're sleeping, or sick—are devoted to being active. And in our obsession with activity, we miss out on the amazing rewards of allowing ourselves to rest and to receive.

Peter Wayne, my t'ai chi teacher, often tells us in class: "Don't just *do* something—stand there." Much of the practice of t'ai chi is learning how to just "stand there." The same is true, I believe, with the practice of writing. If you've been doing the various writing practices, you've become familiar with the active part of writing—putting content on the page with concentration and intention. And have you ever noticed that it's the time after you *stop* writing that you often get your best ideas and insights? If you have, you've been noticing your experiences of "not-doing." I believe that learning how to cultivate such experiences is a very important part of becoming a writer. One way to explain what's going on in these experiences is to say that our subconscious mind is at work. (Some also call it "the Muse.")

HOW TO USE THE SUBCONSCIOUS

We spend most of our time using our conscious mind. We have to: There's so much coming at us all the time in our high-speed world that, if we're not alert, we're in trouble. But you can think of the mind as a bit like an iceberg: The conscious part, the part we are aware of, is only the top of it, the visible surface. And underneath that, in what we call the subconscious mind, lies all the stuff we didn't know we knew.

When you do freewriting and things come to you—ideas or insights, images or information—that you didn't know you knew, that's your subconscious mind at work (in combination with your creative faculty). Just as important is that your subconscious will often continue to give you more "stuff" even after you have stopped your writing practice session. When you can, it's a good idea to leave yourself some time for this to happen and some mental space so that you can pay attention to what your subconscious is giving you.

As you become more comfortable with writing practice, try to get into the habit of leaving yourself time at the end of your sessions so your subconscious can work on the material you have just written. You will want to let your mind stay in the "writing zone," so it's a good idea to turn next to something that doesn't require verbal activity. Don't pick up the phone or check your e-mail; don't turn on the radio; don't start a conversation or pick up a book. Instead, go for a walk or a run, lie down for a few minutes, wash the dishes or walk the dog. Or just sit and stare out the window. You will be surprised, when you do this, at how often some useful idea or insight surfaces in your mind.

Naturally, you'll want to write down whatever comes to you, so if you need to leave your practice place, be sure to bring with you some paper, or a small notebook, and a pen.

PRIMING THE SUBCONSCIOUS

The history of human creativity is filled with examples of people who got their best ideas by first working hard on a problem, then resting. The poet A.E. Housman, for instance, said that he would fill his mind with material for a poem, then take a nap under a tree;

How to Be a Writer

and when he woke up there, in his mind, would be the completed poem. John Updike explained that he would frequently leave his study, where he'd been writing, to sit in his garden and stare at the sky. Often some family member, seeing him apparently doing nothing, would approach and ask him to do some task. "No," he would tell them. "I can't. I'm working." The novelist Louis Bromfield discovered that he could train his subconscious to work while he was sleeping or relaxing.[8] "Very often," he said, "I have awakened in the morning to find a problem of technique, or plot, or character, which had long been troubling me, completely solved while I had been sleeping." These writers knew how to make use of the active-receptive rhythm of creativity, how to make use of both the conscious mind and the subconscious.

The subconscious reminds me of the genie in Aladdin's magic lamp: Just ask and it will give you anything you want. You have to know how to ask, though. If you want your subconscious to give you gifts, first you have to give *it* something—it needs to be primed to work well. One of the best ways to do this is to do some collecting, using any or all of the writer's faculties.

PRACTICE: Mull Over Your Observations

Go out and do some observation practice and then give your subconscious time to mull over what you observed. Or do some memory or imagination practices, rest, and see what comes up for you. Write down what your subconscious gives you.

PRACTICE: Enter Into a Receptive State

Pick a subject and use focused freewriting to collect material on it, writing for at least ten minutes. (Use whichever writer's powers you choose.) This lets your subconscious know that you want material on this subject. Then lie down or go for a walk or do some household task, trying to stay relaxed and keep your mind in a receptive state. If your subconscious gives you some new material or ideas, write them down.

PRACTICE: Use Procrastination

If you have a tendency to procrastinate about writing, try this: Do some freewriting about your subject without even trying to collect. Write about experiences that made you pick this subject, write down your questions about it, write about how you hate it. It doesn't matter what you write, as long as you get that pen moving. And then, having primed your subconscious with this "junk" writing, you can clean your house or walk the dog or do whatever else you do when you procrastinate. You will likely be pleasantly surprised to find ideas popping into your head.

MAKE TIME FOR THE SUBCONSCIOUS

This doesn't mean, though, that we *must* use everything the subconscious offers us. It simply gives; with our conscious minds we can choose whether or not to use any particular gift. And while the subconscious will work on material you provide it with even at times when you are very busy, if you never slow down enough and make the mental space to hear its voice, chances are good that, like a spurned lover, it will eventually fall silent.

So I encourage you to consider ways you can plan your writing time to make use of the on-off rhythm of creativity, to practice moving back and forth between writing and not-writing until that rhythm becomes comfortable. You might try saving mundane tasks like making the beds until after you have done some writing, so your subconscious can work while you get that task done. Or you might want to prime your subconscious with some collecting before you go out for a run. Making space in your life for your subconscious to speak to you will help you devote more time and mental energy to writing and give you a way to do some of your writing work even when you're not at your desk.

THE CREATIVE CAULDRON

The subconscious is the cauldron where the alchemy of creativity takes place. Just as a cook can simmer a pot of water, vegetables, and herbs and end up with soup, so we can "simmer" images, ideas, questions, bits of information, and so on in the subconscious. Very often what will emerge is something that, like the cook's soup, is more than the sum of the original ingredients. Perhaps we will get a new idea that has somehow fused from a few pieces of information, or a character who combines elements of different people, or an insight for how we might structure a story, or a new image for a poem. There is no telling what our subconscious might come up with if we let it do the work it is designed to do!

As with all the other faculties, if you haven't used your subconscious much, you may feel awkward trying it out. Remember that you are learning a new skill, and give yourself lots of time to practice. Remember, too, that the subconscious works at its own pace and in its own way. After you have given it material to work with, you will need to be patient and wait for it to speak to you in its own time. You cannot command your subconscious to help you; you can only invite its participation. If you practice being receptive, if you make space in your writing life for the subconscious, if you learn to listen to its voice, you will be well rewarded.

CHAPTER 9

Curiosity

> The answer to the question [how to make our writing interest-
> ing] is, that you write interestingly only about the things that
> genuinely interest you. This is an infallible rule.
>
> —TED HUGHES, *Poetry in the Making*

Have you ever found yourself wondering why the sun seems to make
arcs of different lengths in the sky at various times of the year? Or
how many Red Sox players have been American League MVPs? Or
what it's like to live in the Arctic? Or what the relationship is between
the man and the woman you overheard arguing in the subway?

When you wonder about things, when you ask questions to
which you don't yet have answers, you are exercising another writer's
power: curiosity. Like the other writer's faculties, curiosity is a natural human faculty; if you've ever been around small children, you will
have witnessed their seemingly inexhaustible curiosity: *What is that
for? What's the name of that flower? Why is the sky blue?* While adults sometimes feel annoyed by children's endless questions, most of the time
young ones are not trying to be annoying; they just want to *know*.

That's the power of curiosity: the desire to know about something. Our curiosity, then, comes out of *desire*.

Unfortunately, for many of us, our natural curiosity has been
suppressed, sometimes killed off altogether, by years of schooling

that train us *not* to ask questions. The teachers most of today's adults grew up with didn't want us to ask questions—*they* asked the questions; we were supposed to have the answers.

USING YOUR CURIOSITY

Curiosity—the desire to know—is the essential foundation of any real learning. By "real learning" I mean learning that we own, that becomes part of us—unlike the information or ideas that we memorize to regurgitate on an exam, or throw together for a paper, which we then forget as soon as the exam is over or the paper handed in. It's also one of the best ways to build our content-minds: to discover subjects we might want to write about and material we can use in our writing.

PRACTICE: Wake Up Your Curiosity

Take a few minutes to list everything that you can think of that you are interested in or curious about. Keep the pen moving. What do you *want* to know about—or to know more about?

When you're finished, look back through your list and pick the items that stand out for you right now. Any one of these could be a subject you might write about.

When you bring your curiosity to your memories, or to your observations, you can also find potential subjects, or more material on a subject you've begun to write about. Suppose, for instance, you notice during one of your observation "expeditions" that there's a street performer who juggles firebrands as part of his act. As you watch, your curiosity might start to ask questions: *Isn't that dangerous? How does he do it? What would make a person want to do that?* Take note of these questions; perhaps they will lead you to a story or a poem or an article.

Most writers are people who still retain the natural curiosity of children. They ask questions; they want to know. John McPhee, the famous writer for *The New Yorker,* used to buy a glass of orange juice every day from a vendor in New York City. He paid attention and noticed that the juice differed in color from one time to another. Then his writer's curiosity kicked in, and he wondered why that was. Then he started to explore that question, got interested in the subject, and wrote an entire book on the Florida citrus industry. It's not only nonfiction writers and journalists who use their curiosity; fiction writers, poets—any kind of writer—can be led by their curiosity to things to write about. The English writer Edward Rutherfurd became curious about the history of the English town of Salisbury; *Sarum,* the novel that resulted from his explorations into that history, became a bestseller. Jean Auel, a self-described "ordinary housewife," became fascinated by the Stone Age; her first novel, *The Clan of the Cave Bear,* was also a bestseller.

Learn to trust your curiosity—you never know where it will take you. Let yourself wonder about things and write down your wonderings. If you feel that your curiosity needs exercise, I recommend that you do lots of this practice of asking questions. Bring your curiosity not only to your writing, but also to your life. You may never get to explore many of the questions you come up with, but you will undoubtedly find some that attract you enough so that you want to find answers.

We can use our curiosity not only to come up with subjects to write about; we can also use it to begin exploring a subject we have chosen.

PRACTICE: *Explore Your Subject Via* Internal *Collecting*

When we come up with a subject we want to know more about, we might assume that our first step must be going off to find out things about it. But it's far more helpful to take a different step first: Start by finding out what you already know about your subject.

To practice this, select one of the subjects from the list you made of your interests. Then do at least ten minutes of internal collecting on this subject (using the focused freewriting technique): What do you already know about it? What experiences have you had with it? What are your opinions or thoughts about it? And—most important of all—what are your questions about it? What do you *want* to know?

You can also bring your curiosity to material that you have collected using your memory or your power of observation or your imagination. To practice this with memory, read through one of your focused freewriting exercises using memory, bringing only your curiosity to what you have written. Write down all the questions that come to your mind. If you want to engage your curiosity with some observations you have made, or with material that has come from your imagination, do the same thing.

Sometimes after we have done some initial focused freewriting on a subject that interests us, we don't know what to do next. Usually our material needs to be developed in some way, and engaging with it using our curiosity is a powerful way to help that happen. Once we have asked questions of our material, we often see where we need to go next.

Once we have come up with questions of our material, we need to *answer* some—or all—of those questions!

Often we can come up with the answers ourselves. For instance, if a writer has collected material about his grandmother and come up with the question, "Why was she so mean?" he may be able to answer that question from his own experiences and recollections. Or perhaps he wants to use this material to create a fictional character—he can invent an answer that will make the character work. But sometimes we aren't able to answer our questions ourselves. In that case, we need to look outside of ourselves for answers.

THE POWER OF CURIOSITY:
THE TRUTH ABOUT RESEARCH

Let me tell you a true story. Once there was a young woman I'll call Susan—a bright young woman a couple of years out of graduate school in theology, where she had written lots of research papers. Susan came from a small town in Ohio, but she was living in Boston when the Episcopal Church began to consider the issue of gay marriage. Susan's mother was still living in that small Ohio town, and still attending the Episcopal church there, which Susan also had attended. The minister of that church was adamantly opposed to gay marriages. Susan's mother wasn't sure she agreed with him, so, figuring that her daughter's education must have given her an edge, wrote her a letter asking for help in discussing the issue with the minister.

Susan was delighted to be asked, flattered that her mother wanted her help—and paralyzed by anxiety over how to answer. Some of that anxiety had to do with the fact that she knew her mother would be sharing what she wrote with their minister. But she also wasn't sure how she herself felt about the issue, and she didn't feel confident that she could come up with anything helpful to say to her mother. She tried doing internal collecting, but that didn't help. And then she had a revelation.

As she told our writing group, "I realized I could go to the library and do some research on this issue! Then I'd feel confident in what I have to say." She shook her head in amazement at how long it had taken her to come up with this solution. "I wrote so many research papers when I was in school," she said. "But it just didn't occur to me that I could do research on something that I *wanted* to know about."

I wish I could say that Susan's story is unique; but, alas, I know that it isn't. Students typically do research for papers because they have to, not because they want to; like Susan they may assume, consciously or not, that research is something one does only in school—a purely academic exercise, not something one would do for one's own purposes.

What a tragedy this is! For finding out things that we *want* to know is one of life's great pleasures. To experience this pleasure for yourself, first start by bringing your power of curiosity back to life through one or more of the practices of asking questions.

Then, if you can't answer your questions yourself, start looking outside yourself to discover answers. Not the "right" answers—the answers that satisfy your curiosity, the answers you need for yourself and, if you are writing for others, for your piece of writing. In searching for these answers you will be engaged in external collecting. Inexperienced writers, having been instructed so often to "write what you know," often assume that anyone who writes on a subject, using information outside of her own experience, must have somehow known that material already. One of my students shared her surprise, in browsing through the acknowledgments in books she read, to discover the writer giving thanks to "Mary, who taught me about otters," or "John, who explained particle physics." "I always assumed that a writer always knew all of that stuff already," she said. "I never realized you could actually *learn* things to write a book."

"Learning things" is what most writers do. So they do lots and lots of external collecting—not just the collecting of sensory details, as in the observation exercise, but odd bits of information, curious facts, how things work—anything that catches their fancy. And when a writer's curiosity leads her to a subject she wants to write about, then random external collecting leads to a deliberate search for material—research.

Research is just another name for external collecting driven by your curiosity rather than your power of observation. And when you are looking for something because you *want* to, rather than because you have to, then research can become an adventure.

PRACTICE: *Explore Your Subject Via* External *Collecting*

Pick a subject that you want to know more about, and collect your questions. Now examine these questions, one by one and think about how you can go about getting answers. Do you have a simple question of fact that you can answer by looking up your subject in an encyclopedia or some reliable online source? Or do you have more general, exploratory kinds of questions? Consider your possible resources. Where might you go to find the answers you need? Perhaps you will start with other people. If, for instance, you think your mother will have information or ideas for your piece about your grandmother, you can simply ask her for them. You might even want to write out your questions in advance and interview her.

If you like to talk to people, you may want to practice doing some interviews. Most people enjoy talking about themselves, whether it's telling stories about their lives or sharing information or expertise. A vast number of nonfiction books are based at least in part on interviews. Even fiction writers can do interviews: A novelist I once knew had decided that a main character in a book she was working on had to be a veterinarian; so, knowing nothing about the subject, she found a veterinarian and interviewed him to gather material for creating her character. Best-selling novelist John Grisham claims to loathe research, but he collects material for his books by interviewing lawyers.

PRACTICE: Use the Interview to Expand Your Knowledge

For this exercise you will need a partner. One of you will take the role of the interviewer, the other the role of the person being interviewed; after you have done the exercise once, exchange roles. The person who will be interviewed needs to come up with a few subjects which he knows something about and present this subject list to his partner. She gets to decide which topic on the list she wants to learn something about, and should ask herself, *What would I like to know about this subject?* She then spends some time writing down interview questions. Using these questions as a guide, she will then interview her partner, writing down his answers to her questions, as well as anything else he says about the subject that interests her.

An interview is not just a polite conversation; it's an exercise in using your curiosity. Good interviewers try to ask questions that will lead the person being interviewed to expand on basic factual statements and simple "yes" or "no" answers. An interviewer is trying to collect lots of material to work with, so if you are playing that role, you will want to keep your curiosity engaged as you listen to your partner talk. Let it stay alert for things she or he says that make you think of new questions, and then ask those questions. Naturally, you don't want to push someone into talking about things he clearly doesn't want to talk about; you just want to stay interested and keep showing that interest by asking more questions, either during this interview session or at another time.

If you want to go further with this exercise, then read through all the material you have collected, and write down any new questions you have. Get more answers, ask more questions ... until your curiosity is satisfied. If you like this practice, you may want to find other people to interview.

THE ADVENTURE OF RESEARCH

Doing research is a journey of exploration. Like any journey it has times of exhilaration, and times of frustration. But if you let yourself be guided by your curiosity—if you are genuinely interested in your subject—most of the time it's a wonderful adventure. There's a vast world of potential resources out there: people, books, magazines, tapes, Web sites, and more that can provide answers to your questions. Give yourself time to explore the resources that can help you on your particular quest—remember, you don't have a deadline, so you don't have to rush—and you will probably be amazed at what you find. If you've never before had the opportunity to do research in this way, here are a few suggestions to get you started.

GET AN OVERVIEW OF YOUR SUBJECT

Once you've done some internal collecting to find out what you already know and what your questions are, you might want to get some kind of overview of your subject. Some writers seeking an overview head for the Internet or an encyclopedia. Many others go to their local library, find the section where books on their subject are shelved, and just browse. You can do the same in bookstores (which gives you an excellent reason to go to a bookstore!). Asking for help from your local library's reference librarian can also get you started.

Remember that this is your own journey, and you can take it any way you like. There are no deadlines you have to meet, no professors to tell you you're doing it wrong. And there are no academic committees creating artificial boundaries between subjects. If your exploration takes you into literature and then into history and then into science and then back to literature, great! And if you find an attractive side road that branches from the highway you started off on, and you want to venture down it, by all means, do. Go where your own need to know takes you.

CHOOSE YOUR NEXT STEPS

Once you have an overview of your subject, if you've decided to begin there, then you can decide which part of your subject you want to explore first. If you are fascinated by Antarctica for instance, do you want to explore the climate and topography first? Or the creatures who live there? Do you want to read a biography about one of the expeditions to this continent? You get to choose!

You also get to choose the kind of book about your subject that you want to read. If you are approaching a subject for the first time, I highly recommend that you start with books for children or young adults. They usually do a great job of giving basic information about a subject; they are almost always much better designed than adult books; and they are often full of fabulous illustrations. (Many of us are visual as well as verbal learners.) Above all, look for books that are well written. In general, try to avoid anything written by academics: Their writing is usually terrible, and far too many of them can make even the most fascinating of subjects seem quite dead. When you find a book that looks interesting and read it, or part of it (you don't have to read the entire thing— there won't be an exam!), there may be other books mentioned in the text, or there may be a bibliography, and one of those books may show you your next step.

It's true that the initial stages of a learning journey can feel confusing—*Which books should I read? There's too much material!*—and if you find this confusion too hard to cope with, you may want to take a course in your subject. (There are teachers who can impart what they know with passion and clarity.) But if you enjoy the process of discovery—which is, after all, what real learning is all about— then I urge you to stick with your learning journey through the early confusion. You don't have to read everything. You can skim a book, or look through the table of contents or the index to see if it contains material that will be of value to you. Sometimes looking at the book's bibliography can tell you whether it's something you want to read right now. And you can always take note of books that look interesting but which don't seem right for you at the moment.

When you're on a learning journey, it's essential to remember that, as with a journey on foot, you can take it only one step at a time. That means you need to be aware of what you really need at every stage of your learning journey. When we take conventional classes, the teacher decides what we should be learning and in what order. But not everyone learns in the same way, and what makes sense to a teacher may not make sense to you. When you take your own independent learning journey, *you* get to decide what you need to learn next. At first, if you have never done this kind of learning before, you may feel overwhelmed by all the possibilities. Writing can help you sort through them and keep your feet on your own path.

When we take classes in school, most of the time we don't do any writing until the end of a course or a section of it: then we write a paper; we take a midterm or a final exam. So we are conditioned to believe that we really can't do any writing until we've already learned things; we have to "know" the material before we can write about it. How wrong this is! For writing, far from being just a way to present what we already know, is one of the most useful tools there is to help us learn.

USE WRITING TO LEARN

Now that you are comfortable with doing practice writing, you will find it easy to use writing in this way. When you have found material on your subject that satisfies your curiosity—from printed sources or from the Internet, from a person or from a tape—you may want to collect some of it. One way to do this is to take notes. If you do a lot of this kind of external collecting, you will need to devise a system for managing all your collected material. Some people like to use note cards; others like to take notes on the computer. In the past I used notebooks, with each notebook dedicated to one subject. I usually wrote on only one side of the page so that I could make comments on the reverse side, if I wanted to. A notebook also gave me a place to paste in clippings or notes I'd made on scraps of paper. (A file folder would work just as well.) Now, though, I keep my notebooks in files on my computer; I take time every so often to type in the notes I've made on scraps of paper.

When you are doing external collecting from published sources, such as books, articles, or Web sites, there are a couple of common-sense things you need to do. First, you need to make sure you write down enough information about your source so that you can find it again if you need to. (For a book, that's usually the author, the title, the publisher, and the date of publication.) Then, when you take notes, you need to make sure that you write down where each bit of information comes from, so that you can find it again if you need to, and so that you can let your reader know where you got it, if you end up writing something for an audience that is based on your research.

You can take notes in two ways: by copying out a passage word for word, in which case you need to use quotation marks around the passage, or by putting the information the passage contains in your own words. In both cases, you should also write down the page number of the book or article where you found the passage.

PRACTICE: Learn by Writing

Most of you are probably familiar with these techniques of note taking. But writing can do much more to help you learn! Try this: After you have collected some information about your subject, do some freewriting about what you have just learned. There are two parts to this freewriting. First, write down everything that you learned, repeating or summarizing any information you've already made note of. Then reflect on what you learned. Write down what you think of the material you've just read: Do you agree with the author? Does this material fit with other things you have learned so far about your subject? What new questions do you have now? This kind of reflection helps you see what you have truly taken in from your source; it helps you integrate the material in a way that just taking notes can't do; and it helps you get a sense of where you might want or need to go next.

PRACTICE: Bring in the Subconscious

Once you have done some external collecting and (if you like) some reflection, give yourself time for your subconscious to work on your material. In fact, you may want to set up a routine for doing research in which you collect, then rest so your subconscious can work on what you have collected, and then do some focused free-writing on your subject. You will probably be amazed at how much you have learned!

PRACTICE: Bring in Your Imagination

You may also want to bring your imagination into this learning process. At first making use of the imagination as a learning tool may feel strange to you. In this culture, the imagination has been banished from most academic settings in favor of the intellect. The intellect is certainly a useful human faculty—but it is not the only way to know, not the only way to learn. Our imaginations can give us a kind of knowledge of a subject that is even more powerful and useful than that provided by the intellect. So, if you like, after you have done some research on your subject, see if you can find a way not just to think about what you have learned, but to *imagine* it. For instance, suppose you are reading about Antarctica. Can you imagine, using all your senses, what it would be like to be there? Can you imagine what it felt like to be one of the early Antarctic explorers, like Shackleton or Amundsen, or what it would be like to tag a penguin for scientific research? You might want to play with what your imagination gives you by writing it down: Create a description that will help someone feel the cold, or write a story about an explorer—or what it might feel like to be that tagged penguin.

Letting your imagination collaborate with your curiosity in such ways will help you learn about your subject in far more interesting and fruitful ways than the academic approach usually provides. You will probably feel that you truly *own* your material.

PRACTICE: *Share What You Learn*

Another way to make a subject your own is to tell other people about what you are learning—your friends, perhaps, or your friends' children. When you have to explain something to someone else, you are forced to make it clear for yourself. (Albert Einstein once said, "If you can't explain what you know to a five-year-old, you don't really know it.") Perhaps you will even be able to find an opportunity to teach what you know; there's no better way to learn a subject than to teach it! When learning is an adventure, we get excited about what we are learning, and we want to share our learning with others. Look for opportunities to do that: Perhaps you might want to volunteer to talk about your subject at an elementary school or at your church or at a homeless shelter.

You can also use writing to reflect, not only on the material you are collecting, but on your own learning process. How has your learning journey gone so far? What do you sense your next steps might be? Might you want to make an informal list of the books you want to read next or the particular areas of your subject you want to explore? When you take the time to do such reflection you are taking charge of your own learning: You are making your own learning plan—your own curriculum—which you can change whenever you wish.

 ## Tips for Research

- Research is a journey into unfamiliar territory. It's always a good idea to start by identifying where you are are now. Use internal collecting to get a sense of what you already know about your subject and what you want to find out.

- If you are the type of person who likes to plan every detail of a trip in advance, you may want to make a similar kind of plan for your research journey. If you prefer to just embark on your journey and find your way as you go, that's fine, too.

- It's a good idea to take notes of where you travel on your journey: the books you've consulted, the Web sites you've visited, and so on. That will keep you from wasting time exploring resources you've already visited.

- Unless your journey of research is one in which you are actually going to a place or talking to people, you will be relying on written sources. You need to make sure that the sources you learn from are reliable. Look at the author's credentials and expertise. Check that her book lists the sources she has used. The more you get into your research, the more you will be able to decide whether a given author knows what she is talking about.

- Another way to establish the reliability of sources is to befriend a good research librarian at your local library. You can also find a list of reliable online resources at this site: www.ipl.org/index.html. (This site is the result of a merger between the Internet Public Library and the Librarians' Internet Index.)

THE PASSIONATE LEARNER

As a practicing writer you can go on a learning journey whenever you want to, and I urge you to do so. The more you practice doing research motivated by your curiosity, the more confident you will become in your ability to find answers to your questions. And, as with the observation and memory and imagination practices, anything you collect through research may surprise you someday by turning out to be just the thing you need for a piece of writing you hadn't even conceived of when you were doing that research. Even more important, the more you collect, the more you know—and that knowledge becomes an ever-deepening river from which you can draw material to use in your writing. Good writers are writers who have educated themselves in many areas, not just through personal experience.

Your curiosity may lead you to subjects you never expected to be interested in. A few years ago, I began to explore the history of the English language. I had no idea that I would be seduced into learning about English history as well. But once I learned about the Anglo-Saxon origins of our language, I found myself wanting to know more about the people who spoke what we call "Old English" and about how they lived. Soon I had collected a pile of books on the Anglo-Saxons from the children's room of my local library. After a while I was ready for some nonacademic adult books on the subject and was becoming familiar with Anglo-Saxon kings like Offa, who had an earthen dyke built on the boundary between England and Wales, a wall that can still be seen today, and Harold, who lost the famous Battle of Hastings that allowed the Normans to conquer England.

A learning journey can go anywhere you like. One of my students researched his ancestry and discovered he is distantly related to Oliver Cromwell. One woman got interested in the writing of May Sarton and decided to read all her novels. Another woman was planning a first trip to Gettysburg and decided to do some research beforehand so she would get more out of her trip. Always, by its nature, a learning journey is active learning, not the passive kind one undergoes watching an educational television program or in many classrooms. Active learning gives you the thrill of discovery when you find out something you never knew before, and the pride and pleasure of ownership of this knowledge, because you found it for yourself.

Becoming an active learner can transform your writing, expanding its horizons far beyond the limits of your personal experience. More than any other activity, exercising your curiosity through active learning will build your content-mind and fill it with potential material. Perhaps even more important, this activity can transform your life. When you practice coming to the world with your curiosity, your desire to know about a particular subject may flame into a passion for being a learner, a passion that can lead you places you never dreamed of going: to a foreign country, perhaps, or (in your imagination) to a time in the past, to a new career or volunteer work, or to a pursuit that sustains you in retirement. That passion—far more than the accumulation of material goods our culture insists we need—can lead you to your real interests, to your authentic self.

When we're engaged in passionate learning—just as when we're passionately in love—we feel excited, we feel fully alive, we feel more interesting to ourselves and to others. And while a love affair may not last, as writers we can be passionate learners for our entire lives.

CHAPTER 10

The Sherlock Holmes School of Writing

You see but you do not observe.

—Sherlock Holmes to Dr. Watson,
A Scandal in Bohemia

Sherlock Holmes, the famous fictional detective, wrote only rarely for publication about his cases; he left the writing to his friend Dr. John Watson. But in solving the strange and complex crimes that came his way, Holmes regularly used all of the writer's powers you've been experimenting with. He astonished Dr. Watson at their first meeting by telling the good doctor, quite correctly, "You have been in Afghanistan, I perceive."[9] Close and precise observation was the foundation of Holmes's method. Then he would draw his inferences based on those observations. (As he later explained to Dr. Watson, he observed him closely when they were introduced, noticing that Watson's face was tanned, though his wrists were pale, and that he was holding his arm stiffly as if it had been injured. From these and other details Holmes rapidly concluded that Watson had been a medical doctor in Afghanistan, where English troops were then engaged.)

When inference alone did not suffice, Holmes would search his memory for expertise he had acquired which would give him the information he needed. Though Holmes never graduated from college, he educated himself in the areas he knew would help him in his work: He made chemical experiments; he carefully studied footprints; and he made a scientific study of pipe, cigar, and cigarette tobaccos, so that he could identify at a glance a bit of ash left behind at a crime scene. He was a relentless collector of information about people and things, and had in his sitting room what amounted to his own personal encyclopedia. So, for example, when the King of Bohemia came to consult him about the adventuress Irene Adler, Holmes had only to look into his files to find her biography "sandwiched between that of a Hebrew rabbi and that of a staff-commander who had written a monograph upon the deep-sea fishes."[10] And when he did not have the information he needed already, Holmes knew how to direct his curiosity to give him the right questions; and he knew how to do research—at a newspaper office, for instance—to get the information he needed.

Holmes also knew how to use his imagination to put himself in the place of the criminal and imagine how he or she had proceeded. Imagination, he often remarked, was essential to a good detective, and he scorned the Scotland Yard detectives who frequently consulted him for their lack of it.

No one who has read any of the Holmes stories can fail to notice that Holmes knew how to use his subconscious. Time after time Watson describes him as withdrawing into a kind of waking dream-state, half-dozing on his couch or idly scratching at his violin. And it was after he had meditated in this way upon all the material his other faculties had given him that he would suddenly come to himself and state—to his friend's amazement—"Ah, Watson, I have it now."

Though not a writer himself, Holmes is a model of a person who kept his powers sharp through constant exercise, and who knew how to bring them together to solve particular problems. (Apparently Sir Arthur Conan Doyle, Holmes's creator, based him on a real person—Dr. Joseph Bell, a surgeon in Edinburgh who had been one of Conan Doyle's teachers in medical school.)

How to Be a Writer

As you gather and develop your own material, you will naturally use more than one of your powers. You may also enjoy the following practice, a writing "game" inspired by Sherlock Holmes, to get you in the habit of allowing your different powers to collaborate.

PRACTICE: Be Sherlock Holmes: Use All Your Powers

Begin with making some observations in a particular place. (Write them down in your notebook.) Then consider, on paper: What do your observations tell you about the people or things you are observing there? (For instance, if you notice that a person on the street is walking very fast, you might conclude that he is in a hurry, perhaps late for an appointment.)

Now search your memory and your expertise for information that might tell you more about whatever it is you are observing. Bring your curiosity to bear as well: What questions come to your mind about what you have observed? How could you answer them? (Perhaps the man is smoking a cigarette; perhaps that makes you wonder how many people still smoke; perhaps when you get home you will do some research on the Internet to see if you can find the answer to this question.)

You can also bring your imagination to your observations. What does your imagination want to do with the details you've collected?

Once you've allowed your faculties to collaborate in this way, let your subconscious take over for a while. Let your mind rest and give it a chance to take in everything you've given it. Then come back to your notebook and do some writing—see what happens. You can let the writing go anywhere it wants; or, if you've gotten an idea for a particular direction you'd like to explore, keep your writing going in that direction.

The goal here is not to come up with a finished piece of writing—though that may happen—but to get used to what it can feel like to allow your writer's faculties to collaborate.

SECTION 3
moving toward readers

CHAPTER 11

Tools for Developing Your Material

Writing, like life itself, is a voyage of discovery.

—HENRY MILLER

About halfway through a writing workshop, students often say things like, "Now I can sit down and write for fifteen or twenty minutes on a subject I've chosen, and I really enjoy it, and I like what I come up with. But I don't know what to do next."

I reply, "Well, now you've gotten to the point in your learning where you need to learn how to *develop* a piece of writing."

I like to think of all the collecting we do in our notebooks—the bits of information, observations, imaginings, ideas, and so on—as a kind of scattering of seeds over the ground. Not all of these "seeds" will germinate, so we need to spread a lot of them. And of the ones that do germinate, not all will develop into finished pieces. Just as tiny plants need sun and water to grow, so our small beginnings need a particular kind of attention from us in order to develop.

Some of you may feel that you and your writing are not ready for this next step. Perhaps you feel that right now you simply need to fill page after page in your notebook with material. Perhaps you feel that all you want to do is to develop your powers through the various practices outlined in the last section. If that's the case, I urge you to trust your writer's intuition. You have the rest of your

life to become a writer, so there's no point in pushing yourself to turn out finished pieces of writing if you're not ready.

On the other hand, perhaps you have been feeling frustrated at your inability to get past that first step of focused freewriting/collecting on a subject. This chapter will give you some ideas about what to do next.

When you want to develop some of your material it's crucial to remember that writing is a *process*. Many students have told me that their mental picture of how writers work comes from Hollywood movies: There the writer sits by a swimming pool, chain-smoking cigarettes and typing madly. His words flow ceaselessly from beneath his flying fingers; in the next shot, the stack of typed sheets beside him becomes, with nary a correction, a stack of best-selling novels.

This fanciful picture has made many would-be writers assume that to be a "real" writer is, necessarily, to write like this, to follow the "get-it-right-the-first-time" model of the writing process I described earlier. Most of us, though, are better served by a different model—one that sees writing not as something we do all at once but as a process that happens in stages. Professional writers know this: They often write many drafts before getting to one that satisfies them. But they don't *publish* these drafts, so all we ever see is the final product. It's easy to assume, as so many beginning writers do, that if you are a "real" writer, you must be able to get to your final draft on your first try.

I urge you to give up this assumption: It just isn't true! Real writers know what they are doing when they write. They understand the process, and they know how to help a piece develop. These are skills anyone can learn; all it takes is time and practice.

ENGAGING WITH COLLECTED MATERIAL

Anytime you pick a subject and collect material on it, through internal collecting or external collecting, or both, you are taking the first step in the writing process. After collecting, your next step is to make choices from all the material you have collected—to decide on the specific bits of material you want to use—and to see what else occurs to you. Here's where your critical faculty comes in: It helps you make these choices. At this stage, you are still developing content, so keep your attention on your material—your ideas, your information, your images—and not on your words.

Before you start making choices, it can be very helpful to have some time away from the "stuff" you've collected so that your subconscious can work on it. Then you can return to your material with fresh eyes. You may discover at this point a reluctance to take another look at your collected material. If so, you're not alone.

Because our writing has so often been evaluated and graded, many of us have internalized that particular way of responding to writing; we may bring to our own written words only our judging minds. Whenever we read over what we have written, our first impulse may be to stamp out what is "bad," to correct, to edit. (I have watched students, in a frenzy of stamping out the "bad," try to obliterate words by scratching pen marks through them over and over until there is a hole in the paper.) But when all you have on the page is merely focused freewriting—just some collected material—you do not have finished text, so there is absolutely no point in judging and editing it.

It's vastly more helpful (and much more fun) to take a non-judgmental attitude towards your focused freewriting/collecting, looking for material you can use and develop further. Instead of evaluating your writing, you *engage* with it. In the process, you will discover which pieces of your material you want to keep, and you will get ideas for developing those bits and pieces into a finished form. When you can approach your collected material in this playful spirit, you will soon overcome your reluctance to reread it.

The following practices are tools to help you engage constructively with material you have collected. Try them all, and then continue using whichever ones work well for you.

1. SELECT

As you read through your collected material, without judgment, do two things. First, mark anything that stands out for you: a word, a phrase, an image, an idea, a piece of information—anything. You're looking for whatever seems to have some energy in it, whatever seems to call out to you, *"Me! Use me!"* Second, notice the new ideas or images that surface in your mind as you read through what you have written, and write them down. (Write in the margins, if you wish, or on another sheet of paper.)

Now take a few minutes to reflect: What did you notice in doing this? What ideas do you have now for developing this piece?

2. QUESTION

Try coming to your collected material with your curiosity. Read through everything you've gathered on your subject, as well as any new material you added if you tried the selecting practice. This time, engage the material with your curiosity, and list every question that comes to your mind. These questions might have to do with the material itself: *What color were Grandmother's eyes? Why did Uncle Albert throw the cat into the lake?* Or they might have to do with how you want to develop your material: *Do I need more description of the lake? Should I have more dialogue?* Keep your pen moving. Trust your curiosity and your writer's intuition to supply you with questions.

When you're done listing questions, take a moment or two to relax, and then go back through your list and mark all the questions that seem interesting or helpful to you. Then pick one or two of them and try to answer them using the freewriting technique.

3. Focus

One of the things that may happen as you do these exercises is that you realize what you are really writing about; in writer's terms, you find your *focus*. Sometimes your focus comes when you realize that you were trying to cover a subject much too broadly; now you want to explore only one piece of it. Sometimes you find your focus when you realize that what you thought you were writing about isn't your real subject at all. Perhaps, for instance, you thought you were writing about childhood experiences of horseback riding, and then you realize that what you really want to write about is the woman who taught you to ride.

One way to find your focus is to "frame" your material: Imagine that you have a picture frame, and you must choose the material that will go inside the frame and let go of the material that doesn't fit. Another way to find your focus is to make yourself state it, in writing. Finish this statement: *What I'm really writing about here is ...* Now ask yourself, "Is this really what I want to be focusing on? Is this topic too big, or too small for the kind of piece I'm ready to write?" Any given subject can provide material for a number of different pieces, each with its own focus.

Another useful technique for finding focus is the mapping technique described on pages 213-214 in chapter seventeen.

4. Picture

You can also bring your imagination to your collected material. After you have selected some material to work with, see if you can make mental pictures of the various things you have collected and play with them in your mind. Your imagination will probably be able to give you more details about a person or a place or an event. You can also try mentally moving the images around, experimenting with different orders. Or you might like to take one "seed" image or piece of information and let it generate more pictures, perhaps even an entire story, in your mind.

You can also use your ability to make mental pictures to envision your entire piece of writing. Perhaps you will arrive at some key images that your writer's intuition tells you are the beginning and end of your piece. Perhaps you will see in your mind a certain shape that your piece wants to take. If you're a visual person, you may want to draw a picture of what you imagine your finished piece might look like.

After you've tried any of these picturing experiments, take some notes about what you've discovered.

5. CONSIDER GENRE

You can take the same material and use it in different kinds of writing, known as *genres*. Fiction and nonfiction are two broad genres. Every genre also has subgenres. For example, romance and mystery are two of the subgenres of fiction. Knowing what genre you'll use the material for can help you both focus and develop your piece. Try asking yourself, "What do I want to make with this material I've collected? A poem? An op-ed piece? A novel?"

If you prefer, you can question your material more directly. Try answering this question, on the page, using freewriting: *What kind of writing does this material want to become?* There is no right answer here, so just trust your writer's intuition. Or you might like to try letting your material answer the question in its own voice: *I want to become...*

If you sense that your material wants to take shape in a genre that you are not very familiar with, you will need to learn more about that genre. Read books in the genre, find how-to books that will give you some instruction in that particular kind of writing, or find a good teacher.

And, as always, remember that you are *learning* as a writer. If your material wants to become a short story, and you've never written one before, go ahead and try. It's the best way to learn. Instead of struggling to write a good story, give yourself permission to write a *bad* one, to find out what you can learn about the genre of story and about yourself as a writer.

6. LEARN

Perhaps you want to ask yourself (or your material), *What do I need to learn in order to write this piece?* Another question that you may find helpful is: *What does this piece need me to do now?* Again, take a few minutes to freewrite an answer. Perhaps now you need to gather some additional information through some form of external collecting. Perhaps you need to bring your imagination to what you've written so far and let it give you more pictures. Perhaps you need to learn something about writing dialogue. Perhaps you need to just sit down and write a draft.

7. PLAN

To plan, or not to plan: That is the question. Some writers hate planning a piece—they get an idea or a character or a setting and just begin writing. There are other writers who make a plan for every piece they write, so that they know where it's going. And it's also possible to combine the two approaches: You can make an overall plan while letting each section find its own way, or you can start out with no idea where the piece is headed, then, once you discover its shape, make an outline. You may want to experiment with writing with and without a plan to see which way best suits you and your writing projects. For some kinds of writing, the technique of making a "map" of your piece (described in chapter seventeen: Getting It Written) can be very useful. You may also want to take a look at "Plan Your Project" on pages 209-210.

8. TAKE YOUR TIME

How long does it take to develop a piece of writing? That depends. I've read of poets who spend ten minutes collecting material for a poem and then write it. On the other hand, the poet Stanley Kunitz once remarked in an interview that he had an idea for a poem when he was quite young and didn't write the poem itself until he was over ninety.[11]

It's very easy to get ideas for pieces of writing—as you practice using your writer's powers, you will discover ideas everywhere—but you may not be ready to write all those pieces yet. Perhaps you're not ready to tackle a certain subject right now. Or perhaps you don't have the technical skills that you need to do justice to your idea in words. One of the advantages of keeping a writer's notebook is that, even if you can't write a particular piece right now, you can save the idea or the materials in your notebook until you're ready to develop them.

Developing a particular piece of writing may not take you a lifetime, but it's likely to take more time than you expect. The process of collecting material, interacting with it, and selecting from it is one you can—and often should—repeat many times. That's because this ongoing engagement with one's own material is absolutely central to the writing process: It is, in fact, at the heart of the work of writing. We've been taught to believe that writing is all about cultivating inspiration and waiting for its magic to descend upon us. There can certainly be times when we are in a state of inspiration, but I believe they come only when we are truly prepared for them. And one of the ways that we can prepare is by getting to know our material very well.

As you interact with your writing, you may discover that you need to do more collecting (internal or external or both) on your subject. Don't be dismayed. That's a good thing; it's part of the work that will help your piece develop. Most beginning writers don't spend enough time on this activity of getting to know their material, so eager are they to produce a final product. But no matter what kind of writing you are doing, if you want your work to be more than superficial, you must thoroughly get to know your material by developing it. Then you'll be able to write from a place of authority. (The words *author* and *authority* both derive from the same Latin word, *auctor*.) Knowing your material well will give you confidence, and that confidence will impart itself to your readers through your words and make them relax and trust you.

And don't forget that your subconscious will be working on your material while you are doing other things. Be prepared for ideas to come to you at odd times—and write them down! You may want to get in the habit of having a small notebook with you at all times or having a notepad and a pen in every room of your home.

9. ORGANIZE YOUR MATERIAL

So what do you do with all the bits of material you are collecting on your chosen subject, with all the pieces of paper and computer files? You have to find a place to keep it so you don't lose it. Organizing material is a big part of the work of writing, and each person has to find his or her own system. As I wrote earlier, when you're developing a piece of writing, you may want to take your collected material out of your writer's notebook and give it a place of its own: a notebook, a file folder, or a folder on your hard drive. With a complicated project, you may use all three. You may want to visit a stationery or office supply store to buy colored clips and folders and binders and other organizing tools.

Although organizing activities like these may not seem like writing—you're not putting words on paper—in fact they are essential to a writer's work. *Where does this go in my story or poem or essay?* is a question you will have to answer over and over again as you work with your collected material. When you physically organize pieces of paper and computer files, you will be encouraging your mind to think about how the various items you've collected might fit together in your finished piece.

10. Connect

You can think of the process of developing a piece of writing as involving three main activities: gathering collected material into one place (and, most likely, collecting more); selecting from that material; and making connections between the various bits you have chosen. Making these connections is an important part of the work writers do: We have to actively engage with our material, and we have to give the subconscious time to mull it over. We need to be able to answer the question, *How does this all fit together?*

In a way writing is like sewing patchwork: We choose bits of material from different places and then connect them into a whole. Every piece of writing has to be shaped from its material. If you know the kind of piece you want to write—a short story, perhaps, or a personal essay—reading in that genre will teach you a lot about how to shape that kind of piece. Acquiring an understanding of the natural relationship between writer and reader, which we'll explore in the next chapter, will also help you order your material. Another tool for finding connections is the zero draft.

11. Write a Zero Draft

You can spend a long time developing your material. At the same time, you don't want to spend so much time on this activity that you become sick of the whole subject. As with so many other aspects of writing, there's a balance to be maintained. You want to spend enough time with your material so that you can write well about it, while at the same time leaving enough mystery so that you want to find out how it develops.

So how can we know when we're ready to stop collecting and write a draft? Trust your writer's intuition; it will tell you. At a certain point for instance, you may start to feel overwhelmed by all your material: There are too many pieces of paper, too many notes written on scraps (or collected in your mind), just too much *stuff*. This is a good time to put together what some writers call a "zero draft."

Writing a zero draft is a process of selecting what you want from the material you have gathered and putting it all together in a single document. It's a way to separate the material you know you want to use from the material you've decided to let go of. You can do this in various ways. You can, for example, print out all the material you have gathered, and then with a pair of scissors cut out the bits you want to keep and tape them together on blank sheets of paper. (If you are working in a handwritten notebook, you can make photocopies of pages if you don't want to tear them out.) You can cut-and-paste into a new document on your computer. You can work partly with a pair of scissors and partly on the computer. You can also put together a zero draft by looking over all your material and then sitting down and freewriting a draft, without worrying about organization or word choice. You can cut and paste some parts and freewrite others, if you prefer.

While there are lots of paths to get to a zero draft, the goal is the same: to get everything you think you want to use into one place so you can see what you have now. If it helps you to make a tentative plan for your piece, like an outline, go right ahead. If it helps you to try to order your material as you put together your zero draft, then do so; but if you're not ready to do any planning, don't.

PRACTICE: Create Your Own Zero Draft

Using any of the drafting techniques outlined above (or of your own choosing), read through all of the material you have gathered through the collecting and developing practices, and use it to put together a zero draft. Concentrate on content, not language.

What do you notice about the process of doing this? You may want to take some notes about anything you did that you felt made the process go well so that you can use those techniques again.

PRACTICE: Engage with Your Draft

Now give yourself some time away from your draft, as much time as you feel you need so you can come back to it with fresh eyes. When you return to it, remember that this isn't a final draft! The zero draft is simply a tool to help you see what you've got and what's missing in your material. So you don't need to focus on the words and how to fix them. Instead, see if you can relax and simply engage with your material. Try to look *through* the words to the images or information or ideas they represent. You might find it helpful, as I do, to think of your bits of material as building blocks which you are going to select and order.

As you read through your draft (and you can do this more than once), take note of what's there that should stay: *Yes, I need that description of the lake;* or *yes, that's an important point.* Let your writer's intuition tell you what doesn't need to stay: *I've described that cat three times!* And let it also notice what's missing, what you still need to collect information on, imagine, or think out. You may find it helpful to use one or more of the other practices in this chapter as tools for engaging productively with your zero draft.

When you are finished, take a few minutes to write down your thoughts on what you need to do next with this material. Now take a rest or go for a walk and let your subconscious mull over the draft. You may be surprised to find that it gives you new material and new ideas about what you need to do next. Don't forget to write those down!

How to Be a Writer

MAKING CHOICES: THE HEART OF DISCOVERY

What you do next in your process of developing your piece depends on what you learned as you engaged with your zero draft. Perhaps you need to collect more information. Perhaps you need to write entire sections to fill in gaps. Perhaps you need to write a beginning. Perhaps you need to rewrite sections that aren't clear. (Perhaps, for instance, all you have in a particular section are notes; you'll need to write those out in sentences.) The essence of this process is that you are making *choices* about how to develop and use your material. Just as it's the creative faculty that gives you all that possible material, it also helps you decide, not what's good or bad, but what you can actually use. Sometimes beginning writers find making these choices difficult; they don't want to let go of a single word they have written. *But making choices really is at the center of creating a coherent piece of writing.* Yes, you may have written a sentence or an image or a paragraph that delights you—but if it doesn't fit, if it doesn't work in your piece as a whole, it will just distract and confuse your reader, and so, alas, it must go. When my students mourn some bit of writing they know they must eliminate, I advise them to create a place where those bits can be saved—a computer file or a section in a writer's notebook. If you can find a way to honor those things you can't use, you may find it easier to let them go, for now. And—who knows?—you may find a use for them someday.

The heart of writing really is making choices, at all stages of the process. It's not just the inevitable falling in love with some of our words that makes it hard; sometimes it's hard to know *how* to choose. Our writer's intuition can help: It often knows better than our conscious mind what we should do. Equally helpful is knowing a lot about the genre you are writing in: A novel works in different ways than a short story; a poem works in different ways than an op-ed piece. The more you can learn about the form of your chosen genre, the more able you will be to make choices.

Making a choice about genre for your piece will help you order and shape your material. So will answering these two essential questions: *What is this piece of writing really about? What do I want it to say to my readers?*

These questions are important because all writing, in any genre (except, perhaps, experimental, avant-garde writing), must have the qualities of unity and coherence. Readers need to be shown how the various bits of material you have chosen connect with each other. All of those bits must work together to get across whatever it is that you want to communicate.

What your piece is about: That's also known as its *focus*, the center to which everything else in the piece connects. You may find, as you mull over your draft, that you want to narrow the focus of your piece: Instead of writing about an entire vacation trip, for instance, you may decide to focus on one incident.

As for what you want your piece to say to your reader, it does not have to be a "message"; it can be anything you like. Perhaps, for instance, on that vacation trip you went surfing in California, and you want your piece to get across to your readers the thrill of that activity. Or perhaps you are telling a ghost story, and what you want your reader to get is a feeling of being scared. Or perhaps you are writing an op-ed piece, and you want your reader to get a new way of looking at an issue.

When you began your piece, you may already have identified its focus and decided what you want to say. But writing is often, and most happily, a process of discovery: We write to *find out* what we have to say, what we want to communicate. So as you develop your material, keep those two questions in mind; they will help you make choices about what should stay in your piece and what you don't need. Everything that helps get across what you are trying to say, stays; everything that doesn't, goes.

This is the point at which you get to do what I call "wrestling" with the material. You try to find an order for all the different bits of writing you have chosen that will help your piece communicate in the way you want it to. You are constantly faced with questions such as these: *Does this bit stay, or does it go? If it does stay, where do I put it? What connections can I make between all of these different bits?* Working with a computer is a godsend at this stage, because you can cut and paste with ease, trying different orders, copying and renaming files. If you've never before worked on a piece of writing in this way, you may find yourself confused and frustrated at some points. Don't give up! Remember that you are learning something new. I always tell my students, "If you're not frustrated at some points in creating a piece of writing, you're not learning." A great deal of the work of writing is solving problems, and the only way you learn how to do that is to practice. Try one solution; if that doesn't satisfy you, try something else. Let yourself take a lot of breaks so that your subconscious can work on your problem.

As you wrestle with your material—making choices, rewriting, making more choices, rewriting—remember to write whatever you can write *now*. If you can't write the beginning, write the middle; if you can't write the middle, write the end. Remember that to become more skilled at developing a piece of writing, you need to practice that skill. You may want to practice by putting several different pieces into zero draft form without necessarily trying to finish any of them, for now.

The process of making choices for a piece of writing can feel overwhelming: There you are, alone with all those possibilities. So sometimes the best way to make the choices that will help you develop a piece of writing is to emerge from your solitary relationship with your material and invite other people into your process. Sometimes while you are developing a piece, and before you have finished it, what you really need are readers.

CHAPTER 12

Your Relationship
with Readers

The difficulty of literature is not to write, but to write what you mean; not to affect your reader, but to affect him precisely as you wish.

—Robert Louis Stevenson

When you are developing a piece of writing, one of the things that can help is to bring in readers, either imaginary ones or real ones. But you have to be ready to do that. Writing practice, as I've said, is private writing. And even when you write pieces you intend to finish, you may not be ready to show them to anyone else.

To assess your readiness, take a few minutes to freewrite your answer to this question: *When you think about other people reading your writing, how does that make you feel?*

When my class of adult beginning writers did this exercise one night, and I asked for their answers, Sally said, "It makes me feel sick to my stomach." Around the room, heads nodded in agreement. Elizabeth added, "It makes me feel incredibly vulnerable." More nodding of heads. Then Ann spoke up. "I agree," she said, "but I also want to *communicate* with my readers. I have something I want them to get." Gail said, "I want to know if people share my experiences, and if they understood what I was saying."

Our feelings about our readers can be complex. On the one hand, they can intimidate or even terrify us; we may fear their scorn, criticism, and judgments—not only on our writing but upon us as human beings. On the other hand, we have things we want to get across to them. How we respond to a reader can depend on who that reader is: We may feel just fine writing a letter to a friend but freeze up when we have to write a term paper for a professor. How do we make sense of these different reactions? To answer that question, let's first take a closer look at the difference between private and public writing.

PRIVATE VS. PUBLIC WRITING

All practice writing is private. Some of it will always stay private, but some of it may become public. It's important to understand the difference.

If you've been engaged in regular writing practice, by now you have probably realized that freewriting and focused freewriting can be great tools for self-exploration. You may have uncovered some long-forgotten memories or gotten an insight about your own behavior or someone else's. In class one night, after ten minutes of practice writing, one woman was moved to exclaim, "I just had the mother of all epiphanies!"

Such intensely personal writing will probably always stay private; most people are not interested in making public what is of interest only to themselves. And private writing does not necessarily have to be like writing in a journal; I know people who have written stories and poems simply for their own pleasure, with no intention of ever showing them to anyone else.

I have a strong belief in the value of writing as a tool for learning and for enjoyment, and so I am convinced that writing practice is worth doing even if every word we write remains private. Beyond the benefits of insight and pleasure it can give us, private writing provides us with practice putting words on paper and gathering content—skills that we can use if we decide we also want to do some public writing. Doing lots of writing that stays private can give us confidence in our writer's faculties so that we can approach public writing with ease.

What, then, is public writing? At its most basic, it is writing we choose to share with other people, writing that will be read by eyes other than our own.

For some creative writing teachers, public writing is nothing more than private writing that is then exposed to public view. These teachers tell their students, "Write as if no one were ever going to read what you wrote." While this approach purports to encourage truth-telling and courage, it does novice writers a great disservice by blurring the distinction between private and public writing. If we write as if no one were going to read our words, we can't possibly learn the skills we must have if we want to attract readers. Public writing is writing that communicates, writing that transfers information or images or ideas or stories from the mind of the writer to the mind of the reader. We can't communicate successfully if we completely ignore our readers.

We may not know, when we begin to put together a piece, whether we will want others to read it. We may prefer to not think about readers while we collect material and mull it over and even write a first (or second, or third) draft. We can keep our work private for as long as we like. But if we intend to make it public, then at some point in the writing process, we *must* consider our readers. And to do that, we need to understand our relationship with them.

THE RELATIONSHIP BETWEEN WRITER AND READER

When you get right down to the basics, public writing is a transaction between one person and at least one other; it's a *relationship* between writer and reader that resembles the relationship that exists when we talk to someone face-to-face. But in conversation we can use all the resources of nonverbal communication in addition to words: facial expressions, gestures, eye contact, and so on. We can also read the other person's body language; we can notice when he seems to be confused or losing interest. The other person can interrupt and ask questions or demand clarification. When we write, it's easy to forget that there's another person "on the other side of the page," so to speak. But even though that person is not physically present as we write, she affects our writing.

There are two ways to think about how readers affect us as writers. One is the effect that readers (or audience) have on us *as we write*. The other is the effect that we want our writing to have *on our readers*.

Let's look first at the effect readers can have on you as you write. Your answer to the question, "How does thinking about people reading your writing make you feel?" tells you a lot about that effect. In the many years I've been asking this question of my students, I have learned that most people feel some kind of fear, ranging from anxiety to outright terror. Why is this so? For many people, "going public" with writing feels like stripping naked and walking around town; there's that same feeling of exposure and vulnerability. No matter how impersonal the topic, our writing reveals something about who we are. But readers can affect us long before they read our words; they can affect us even as we write.

Sometimes in class I do the following exercise to demonstrate the power audience can have on us as we write. First we do the basic freewriting practice, which everyone knows is private writing. Then I tell them, "Now we're going to freewrite again, and this time you'll *have* to read your writing out loud." Everyone freezes. Their tension and anxiety are palpable. And then I say, "Notice how you are feeling. This is what can happen to us *as we write* when we know our words will be read by other people." When we are in that frozen state created by anxiety and fear, it's extremely difficult to come up with things to say, to think and write clearly and powerfully. Even though readers are not in the room with us as we write, their presence in our minds can affect what happens to us as we write. (And, no, I do not in fact make my students freewrite and read out loud.)

I like to do this exercise because it duplicates exactly the experience many adults have had with writing in school. Writing in school is always public writing. Writing academic papers is writing we *have* to do, and it is writing that someone else—the teacher—is going to read, whether we like it or not. We have no choice about doing this writing or about the teacher's reading it. And not only will our writing be read; it will be evaluated and graded.

It's hard to overestimate the negative consequences that learning to write in school can have on us as writers. Paper after paper, year after year, we have learned by experience that to write means having your work evaluated (often by standards that nobody articulates). When I tell my students, "You're going to have to read your words out loud," they immediately assume that their writing will be *judged.*

Over the years (as I've said earlier), I have been horrified to discover how many people have been the recipients of savagely critical judgments on their writing. Even when we're not writing about ourselves, writing is personal; our words and thoughts feel like an extension of who we are. And when they are treated in this harsh manner, it *hurts.* In my twenty-plus years of teaching writing I have met countless people who were traumatized by comments on their work made by a thoughtless teacher. Many people have also had painful experiences in creative writing workshops, where their beginning efforts were dismissed or "critiqued" to the point where they stopped writing altogether.

We can carry around those critical voices of teachers or parents for a long time, and we can project them onto anyone who might read our work now. We can then assume that, like teachers, other readers have unarticulated standards of "good writing" that we cannot possibly meet. Because we are so used to having our writing judged, even when we show it to a friend we may feel a lot of fear and anxiety.

But the negative consequences of learning to write in school can go far beyond the fear and anxiety that we may experience, even beyond the scars from critical responses to our writing, which we may carry for a lifetime. The real problem is that, in spending so much time writing for teachers, we internalize a writer-reader relationship that simply isn't realistic. That's because, outside the academy, readers are not reading our writing primarily in order to evaluate and grade it; they're just trying to understand what we have to say. Writing for teachers and professors is a perversion of the *natural* writer-reader relationship in which one person is communicating something to another.

At the same time, writing for teachers and professors is unrealistic, not just because they award grades, but because they *have* to read student writing. No matter how bad a paper is, the teacher *has* to read it; that's a big part of what he gets paid for. Out in the real world, most of the time no one *has* to read your writing. Is your memo incomprehensible? Into the trash it goes. Is your short story meandering and purposeless? Ditto. Student writers would, I believe, be much better served by professors who simply refuse to read bad writing, who say, in effect, "I don't have the faintest idea what you're talking about here." (To be fair to the students, they are usually imitating the abysmally bad academic writing they have to read for their courses.)

Perhaps the most damaging lesson we learn in writing primarily for teachers is that, in the writer-reader relationship, the reader holds all the power. Because of the nature of the traditional North American academic system, a teacher or professor usually does hold power over his students. As a result, we learn in school (especially in college) to write, not in order to communicate in the way of our choice with someone who can choose not to read our writing, but to please the reader, to impress him, to say what we imagine she wants us to say, to "get the grade." Paper after paper, what we practice is how to write *for* readers rather than *to* them.

For some people, their experiences with writing in school are balanced by writing they choose to do and choose to share (letters, perhaps, or stories that they write and read to their friends). I've noticed that such folks generally feel much more confident in having their words read by others. But those who have written primarily for teachers usually take what they have absorbed about the relationship between writer and reader—namely, that the reader has all the power—and re-create that relationship with *all* of their readers, whether those readers actually have power over them or not. They assume that readers out in the world are like professors, with the power to pass judgment on their work.

Making this assumption can ruin you as a writer. Let me emphasize this point, one of the most important in this book. First, believing readers have power over you creates all kinds of unnecessary anxiety about writing. Even more crucial, the writer-reader relationship we learn in school is simply not accurate; it perverts the true relationship between writer and reader. Outside of school (and outside the realm of critics, who are just another species of professor), writing is not about pleasing or impressing other people; it's about communicating to them. It's about having something to say and saying it *to* others. In the natural relationship between writer and reader, it's the *writer* who has the power: the power of what she has to say, the power to affect readers with the content of her writing and with her language. The *only* power the reader has—certainly a considerable one—is to stop reading.

RECLAIMING YOUR POWER WITH READERS

If you have been well-schooled in the false relationship between writer and reader, you may not feel that you have any of this power.

Don't despair; you can, with practice, change your sense of what it means to write *to*, rather than *for*, others; you can reclaim your power as a writer. The following material will give you some ideas about how to do that, while at the same time showing you how to use other people to help you develop a piece of writing.

1. TAKE YOUR TIME

We can't communicate well when we feel powerless in a relationship, and the relationship between writer and reader is no different from any other. To reclaim our power in our relationship with readers we can begin by assessing whether on our learning journey as writers we are ready to bring readers to our writing at all. I've had students say, "I don't want to write anything for anyone else's eyes but my own. For now, I've realized, I just need to write in my journal." Some people prefer to work on their skills in private for a long time before they are ready to write with other people in mind. There's no rush. If you need total privacy for your writing in order to practice and develop your powers and your voice and your craft, then take it. If you have been totally devastated by someone's negative comments on your work—or, conversely, feel burdened by people telling you how great it is or pressuring you to excel—doing lots of practice writing that you don't share can help restore your delight in your own images or ideas and your confidence in your ability to put them onto the page.

Many of us are so used to writing for others that it can be a revelation—and a huge relief—to realize that (at least in one part of our writing lives) we don't have to. Having your writing all to yourself allows you to develop a new relationship with it: You can become more comfortable playing and experimenting and discovering. You can explore a variety of subjects and genres. You can try out different voices. Most of all, you can reclaim ownership of your writing.

In school, because writing is so often work we must do rather than work we choose to do, we may never have developed a sense of owning what we write. But we need this sense of ownership to become good writers. Good writers feel a sense of empowerment in relationship to their readers. They know they have things to say; they know they have the ability to communicate and the ability to make things happen inside their readers. It can take a lot of learning and a lot of practicing to get to that confident place. Give yourself the time and the mental space you need.

2. Develop Your Writer's Powers

The best way to gain confidence as a writer is to develop your writer's powers. The stronger your imagination, curiosity, and observational abilities become, the more things you will find to write about, and the more you will find to say about the subjects that interest you. If you let yourself engage fully with your material, without worrying about what others might think of it (or of you), then sooner or later you may get to a point where you *want* to share it with others. If you are full of excitement about things you have observed or imagined or learned, you may find yourself eager to pass those discoveries on to readers. And when you get to that point, then you can choose who you want to have read your writing, not so that they can judge it, but so that they can help you develop it.

3. Choose to Share

I want to emphasize that, with your own writing (unlike school or professional writing) you get to choose whether you want to share it, and with whom. If you prefer, you don't have to share any of your own writing at all. Ever. (Yes, I really mean that.) Just knowing that the decision to share or not is all yours can make you feel more powerful in relation to readers.

At the same time, other people can help you find the things you want to say about your subject. As one workshop participant said in class, "Writing doesn't have to be a solitary pursuit. I run my ideas by my wife all the time, and she often makes good suggestions." One of the things most adults learned in writing for teachers is that we can't show anyone our writing until it is finished; we can't bring readers to our writing until it is totally done. If you're comfortable with this approach, fine. But you may want to consider an alternative: bringing readers to your work-in-progress as a natural part of your writing process. When you do this, other people can help you develop a piece of writing and make its content more substantial. In order for you to take advantage of this approach, though, you may need to change your picture of the writer-reader relationship.

4. ESTABLISH A NATURAL RELATIONSHIP WITH READERS

In order to write well to, rather than for, readers, we often need to reeducate ourselves. We have to give up the false model of the relationship between writer and reader in which the reader has power over the writer. But if the reader is not some looming presence lying in wait to critique and evaluate our writing, then who is he? Sometimes when we write, we have a specific audience in mind—we might, for instance, want to write an article on helping toddlers learn to share their toys, specifically for parents of toddlers; or we might want to write a horror story for lovers of that genre. But whether we have a particular kind of reader in mind or not, one thing is *always* true: A reader, no matter who he or she may be, is someone who is not the writer.

This may sound ridiculously obvious. In fact, though, it's one of the most important things we can learn about writing.

Professional writers take this attitude towards readers: *Hey, reader! Listen to what I have to tell you!* But school-trained writers usually don't have that confidence. Partly that's the result of writing for teachers and professors who intimidate us: It's impossible to feel assertive when we feel intimidated. And it's also because those teachers and professors know far more about our subjects than we ever will. How, then, could *we* have anything to tell *them*? And because these academic readers know so much more than we do, we often jump to the conclusion that they can, therefore, also comprehend everything we write about a subject, whether we have made ourselves clear, or not. In effect, we assume that they can read minds. Alas, no one—not even the most erudite professor—has that skill. This assumption that the reader somehow has the ability to read the writer's mind can get transferred to poems or stories or essays, as well as to professional writing, such as the memo that omits an important piece of information because the writer assumes his readers know what he knows. But in the real world, whether we are writing a novel or a business report, we *are* telling our readers things they don't already know: The whole point of public writing is to give readers something—a piece of information, an idea, a story, an experience—they don't already have.

So it's essential to remember that the reader is not you. One of my teaching mantras is: *Remember that the reader is not inside your head.* The reader is a separate person, out in the world somewhere. If you want to reclaim the natural relationship between writer and reader, your first step is to develop a felt sense of your readers as separate from yourself.

Think about yourself as a reader. Most likely, as you read, you are looking for what the writer has to tell you, what she has to give you. You don't want to have to struggle to understand what she's saying; you want her to communicate clearly. And that's exactly how your readers feel when they read *your* writing. They don't want to judge; they simply want to understand what you're saying without having to work too hard.

This work of communicating what you want to say, of making it clear to another person, is the real work of writing. It isn't easy. Readers persist in getting confused or misunderstanding things we are sure we have explained clearly. Learning how to make sure they understand is an enormous part of what becoming a writer, or becoming a better writer, is all about; and the more we learn about how to do this, the more powerful we can feel as writers.

The first source of our power is our material: Once we have something we want to share with others, we have begun to establish a natural relationship with readers. And once we have settled ourselves into this relationship, we can be considerate toward our readers, doing our best to communicate clearly so they can understand and be moved by what we have to say.

Establishing a natural relationship with readers is simply another writing skill, one that we can learn through practice.

5. PRACTICE USING THE NEW MODEL: WRITE TO READERS NOT FOR THEM

Pick a subject that you have done collecting on; look over your material (and, if you like, develop it using the techniques in the previous chapter). Now pick an audience. This can be a real person, if you like, or an imaginary one. It can be your best friend or your spouse or your cat or your car. The essential thing is that this be someone you feel comfortable and safe sharing your writing with.

Now, visualize your reader in front of you, as if she or he or it were sitting right there. Keep that picture in mind as you write. If you lose it, take a minute to bring it back.

And now, do focused freewriting about your subject directly *to* your reader, as if you were talking to him. Remember that your reader is interested in hearing what you have to say, and she doesn't mind if you ramble or repeat yourself. She doesn't care if your writing is not organized or has spelling mistakes in it; she just wants to listen to you and find out what you have to say on your subject. (One of my students once chose her cat as her audience for this exercise; afterwards she commented, "My cat is such a good listener!") So keep the pen moving, just as you would in any freewriting practice, unless you lose touch with your reader; in that case, take a moment to bring his picture back in front of you and return to talking to him on the page. Use your voice as you write; imagine that you are actually talking to your reader.

Afterwards, take a few minutes to notice (and perhaps reflect upon) what happened as you did this.

Most people find this exercise incredibly freeing. For many it's their first experience ever in letting a reader into their process of writing. They are amazed at how many things they came up with to say *because* they were writing to someone else. Their readers have helped them develop writing on their chosen subjects.

You can think of this practice as a different "mode" of freewriting. The private freewriting and focused freewriting you have done up until now is like *thinking on paper;* this new practice is like *talking on paper.* Both modes are useful. Sometimes we just want to sit alone and think in order to develop our ideas; at other times having a conversation with a friend or a colleague is exactly what we need. But whereas an actual friend may be hard to locate at just the moment when we need to write, an imaginary audience can appear whenever we need one.

The more you do this practice, the more you will begin to experience the natural relationship between a writer and her reader: The writer has something she wants to tell the reader; the reader wants to hear it. The more you practice, the more comfortable you will become with writing *to* someone.

Two separate persons—the writer and the reader—connected for a time by a bridge of words: That is the miracle of writing. And it's also what makes writing so hard. When we write solely for ourselves, writing is easy. After all, *we* know what we mean when we use certain words or say certain things. But those darn readers! They persist in not understanding us, in getting confused. Here's a practice to help you get a feel for what happens inside other people when they read your words.

Once again, imagine your safe audience. This time, though, imagine that you *are* that person. Now take what you wrote in the above exercise and read through it slowly, as if you have never seen it before, still imagining that you are your reader and paying attention entirely to content. You may find that it helps to read your words out loud. Remember that your reader has no interest in fixing mistakes in your writing or criticizing its content; she just wants to understand what you are saying. As she reads through it, record her thoughts and comments. For instance, she might say something like, "That's a good point!" or "I like that description!" or she might wonder, "Could you give some more detail about that person?" or "Why are you saying this here? You seem to be contradicting yourself."

When your reader is finished reading and commenting, become yourself again and take some time to think (on paper, if you wish) about your reader's comments. Then write down all the things you need to add or change in what you have written so that what you are saying will be clear to someone else.

This is another way in which considering readers can help you develop a piece of writing. After you do these practices for a while, you will find that you can, at will, summon up an imaginary reader as you write and talk to him or her on the page. You will find that you start to anticipate a reader's questions, and that you take care to answer them. You will find that when you read over your own work, you wonder, not *Is this good or bad?* but *Would someone else understand what I'm saying? Have I made myself clear enough?* You are now well on your way to becoming a writer who can communicate.

6. Use Real Readers to Help You Grow a Piece of Writing

Are you ready to bring some flesh-and-blood readers into your writing process to help you develop a piece of writing? My adult beginners usually dread this—and I never make anyone do it—but sometimes, perhaps during the last class, they have become comfortable enough with each other, and brave enough, to give it a try. (And then, afterwards, someone always says, "I wish we had done this *sooner!*")

You can do this practice after you have done some collecting on a subject and are wondering where to go next. Find a friend or a fellow writer and just talk to him or her about the piece you want to write. What, if anything, might he know about your subject? What resources might she suggest? What stands out for her in what you are saying? What might he want to know more about? What questions does she have? Take notes as your partner talks, and ask more questions as they occur to you. One of the things my students almost always discover as they do this exercise is that the subjects or ideas they want to write about interest others as well; this discovery often encourages them to continue writing.

Just as you can choose whether to bring readers into your process of developing a piece of writing, you can also choose when you want to do it. Perhaps you want to bring in readers right at the beginning, to help you brainstorm ideas for a piece, as just described. Perhaps you want to bring them in later on, after you have a draft written, so you can find out whether what you intend to say is actually getting through to others. Perhaps you want to bring them in only at the end, to give your piece a final read-though and catch any errors. When you invite readers to your work, *you* are in charge. It's essential to remember that. You can ask people to read (or listen to) your writing in whatever way you think will help you at a particular stage of the process.

And you absolutely must make it clear to your readers what you are asking for. If you give a piece of writing to someone and say, "Tell me what you think," you are leaving yourself open to whatever kind of response that person thinks is appropriate, whether it's what you need or not. And since most people automatically adopt the teacher role when asked to read someone else's writing, what you will most likely get is evaluation and criticism.

If this is what you want, then go ahead and get it. But, as Peter Elbow explains in his book, *Writing with Power*, getting this kind of evaluation (he calls it "criterion-based feedback") on your writing is not terribly helpful. Having someone tell you, "This is good," or "This is bad," doesn't help you develop as a writer. And even if your reader instructs you to make specific changes, such as taking out a passage, such suggestions may still not help.

What *is* helpful is to get what Elbow calls "movies of your reader's mind"[12]—that is, to have your reader tell you exactly what happened inside her as she read or heard your words: what she understood, where she got confused, what questions surfaced in her mind, and so on. Most people have had no experience articulating their experiences as readers, so it's helpful to have specific questions to ask them. Some good questions to ask are:

- *What stands out for you in this piece of writing?* (This can be anything: a word, an image, a feeling, an idea.)

- *What do you hear me saying?* (You want your reader to tell you, as best she can, what she thinks you are trying to get across.)

- *What questions do you still have?*

- *What do you need more (or less) of?*

- *Are there places where you got confused?*

- *What effect did this piece have on you?*

Notice that all of these questions demand that your reader give you specific information about what happened inside her as she read your piece. They do not ask for evaluation or suggestions. You will probably need to make it very clear to your reader that such information is *all* you want. It helps to keep asking for more information after your reader has answered one of the questions. For example, if your reader says, "I was confused by that part where the elf turned purple," you can ask, "What was it about that part that confused you?" You may want to invite the reader to point to the specific passage in your piece that caused the confusion. Most readers are not used to articulating in such detail their experience of reading something, so you may have to prod yours a little. Don't be rude, but do persist! The more information you can get about what your words made happen—or didn't make happen—inside your reader, the better!

As you listen to your reader answer your questions, it's essential to the success of this practice that you do not explain what you meant in your piece or defend how you wrote something. It's hard to keep from doing those things, but the more you do them, the more your reader will clam up. Instead, try to really listen to what your reader says—taking notes helps a lot—and take it in. Remember that the reader is not passing judgment on your work; she is simply saying, *This is what I got. Here's where I got confused.* Get your ego out of the way and just listen. You can learn a lot that will help you communicate more clearly.

Then (having thanked your reader for her time and effort), use the information she gave you to try to read your piece through her eyes. Just as you did with your imaginary reader, go through it slowly and see if you can understand why she had the responses that she did. Chances are good that you will have several *ah-ha!* moments in which you understand how you have confused your reader. Sometimes, though, you read over a passage that confused your reader and, even after trying to see it through her eyes, you think, *This is perfectly clear as it is, she just didn't read it carefully.* That can happen; readers are fallible human beings, after all, and we don't always read as carefully as we could. Remember that what you have collected from your reader is simply information about what she experienced as she read your writing *this time.* Perhaps on another day she would read it differently. Ultimately you, as the writer, get to decide whether to make changes in your piece based on what your reader has told you. If you understand how a particular passage confused or misled her, then you make the appropriate changes; if you are absolutely certain that your writing is clear, then you don't. And if you're not sure, then see if you can find other people to read your piece.

In fact, it's always extremely helpful to show your writing to more than one person, if you can. That way you hear articulated several different readers' experiences of your writing; you get a consensus. If three out of four of your readers all get confused by the same passage, then you have probably not been clear; if it's only one out of four, well, perhaps that one person just wasn't paying attention.

The best way to do this practice is with a writing buddy; you take turns giving a reader's response to the other's work. Having to articulate your experience as a reader is just as helpful as getting response to your own work. You begin to internalize the natural relationship between writer and reader; you stop thinking of the reader as someone who has power over you; you begin to understand what it takes to communicate clearly on the page.

If you enjoy this practice of getting and giving response to writing, you may want to form a writer's group to do this on a regular basis. Many writers these days develop their stories and essays and poems with the help of other writers.

The more you practice using other people to help you develop your writing, the more you will understand the natural relationship between writer and reader. You will feel more empowered in your relationship with readers. You will no longer see them as potential judges and critics but simply as other human beings who do want to understand what you are saying and appreciate your making it clear to them. You will no longer be paralyzed by the effect an audience has on you as you write; rather, you will become a writer who thinks about the effect she wants her writing to have on her readers.

1. When you have a piece of writing you want to share with others, think of it as a gift. What, exactly, does it have to give to them? An exciting plot? Insight into a certain subject? An evocation of a particular time and place? There are many possibilities for what your story or poem or essay can give to others.

2. Who would be a good recipient for this gift? Just as you would consider the tastes of the recipients of Christmas or birthday gifts—would Aunt Mary, age ninety-three, *really* want that video game?—so you can think about the kind of person who would enjoy this particular piece of writing.

3. Where can you find this kind of person? If you are writing for children, perhaps the local elementary school would let you come and read your story to a group of kids. If you are writing a mystery, perhaps you have a friend who loves mysteries who would be willing to read your book. If you are writing about a certain subject, perhaps there's an online group devoted to it whose members might be willing to read your piece.

4. If these readers don't have time to answer a lot of questions, just ask them this one: *What did you like about this piece?*

7. Consider Your Purpose

Good writing, I always tell my students, doesn't just lie there on the page. Good writing makes things *happen* inside readers—inside their minds, their hearts, their bodies. When we do all of our writing in school, it's virtually impossible to have any sense that we can affect readers with our words.

But writing outside the academy is totally different. No matter what kind of writing you are doing, be it a report or a poem, you want something to happen inside your reader as he reads it. You want to move him or her in some way. Perhaps you simply want to add to her store of information on a subject. Perhaps you want to change his behavior. Perhaps you want to change her life.

Another way to develop a piece of writing is to consider the purpose of the piece. Take some time to reflect, on paper, about these questions: What effect do you want this piece to have on your readers? What do you want it to *do* to them? (Make them laugh? Make them cry? Make them shiver with fear?) What do you need to include in your piece of writing to create that effect?

Then, as you work on your piece, keep your purpose in mind. Doing this can help you decide which material you should use and what order to put it in. If you choose to show your work-in-progress to readers, you can ask them how it affected them.

You can also learn about purpose by paying attention to what happens inside you when you read something that affects you. What was it about the writing that made it have that effect?

Writers are a lot like magicians: Once we know how to claim our power, once we develop our skills, we can create spells with our writing—spells that keep readers up until midnight with one of our stories, spells in the form of a poem that moves them to tears, spells in the shape of an essay that changes their lives. Of course, it takes a long time to develop this kind of skill—there's a lot to learn—but it can be done. The first step is to develop your writer's powers, so that you have things to say. The next is to develop a feel for the natural relationship between writer and reader, to practice writing *to* your readers. And you need to learn all you can, through reading or courses, and trial and error, about the form and the particular craft of your chosen genre. Finally, you need to become skilled in the use of language.

A writer's main job is to grab and keep the attention of readers. One way we do that is through the practice of telling stories, which we turn to next.

CHAPTER 13

Telling Stories

> *When a day passes it is no longer there. What remains of it? Noth-*
> *ing more than a story. … Today we live, but by tomorrow today*
> *will be a story. The whole world, all human life, is one long story.*
> —Isaac Bashevis Singer

Telling stories is a good place to start writing to others because when you have a good story, you *want* to share it. We do this all the time on the phone or in person: *Guess what I just heard!* We can take that same natural desire to share a story with others and let it become a writing practice.

Telling stories on the page gives us practice in becoming comfortable with our readers, in learning to write *to* them rather than for them. It also helps us practice ordering our material so that readers will understand the story and so it will affect them the way we want it to. And regardless of the genre in which we may want to write, knowing how to tell a story is a useful skill. If you hope to write fiction or memoir someday, telling stories will give you a good introduction to these genres.

LISTENING FOR STORIES

Stories are all around us. To find them, says Joseph Bruchac, a Native American storyteller and writer, all we have to do is to listen.

As we go about our lives, we need to open our ears and take note when a story comes our way. To train ourselves to notice stories, it's helpful to practice using some common story sources. Sometimes, when we explore these sources, we find stories we like that we can simply retell. We can also gather material from story sources and put it together in different ways to create new stories. In both cases, we get practice in the activity of telling a story.

Experiment with the following six approaches to finding and telling stories.

1. Oral Tradition

Before computers—before the invention of writing and books—humans lived in what we now call oral cultures. Everything they knew could be passed on only through the spoken word, and one of the most important ways of preserving and passing on tradition and cultural wisdom was to tell stories. In fact, in most oral cultures there were professional storytellers, whose job it was to remember important events and people, and tell stories about them. But storytelling did not belong only to professionals: it belonged, as well, to ordinary folks, to adults who sat at night telling stories by the fireside to pass a long winter's evening, to grandparents recounting events of their own childhoods to their grandchildren, to parents and nannies telling fairy tales to sleepy children.

The human brain, I believe, is designed to make sense of the world through story; the telling of stories comes naturally to all of us. We may have lost touch with our ability to make stories, but we can easily recover that ability through practice. One of the easiest ways to practice is to retell a story from oral tradition. In the past, most people would be likely to know only stories from their own cultures. These days, though, stories from all over the planet can be found in books of folktales and fairy tales or on the Web. A trip to your local library will provide you with all kinds of possibilities for stories to tell. Perhaps you are especially interested in a particular kind of tale, like traditional ghost stories or tales from Native America. Or perhaps you prefer to begin with an anthology of tales from many different cultures, like Jane Yolen's *Favorite Folktales From Around the World*.

Find a tale you like, and read it over several times until you feel that you know it. Now, run through the tale in your imagination, making pictures of the events. When you're ready, sit down and tell the tale on the page in your own words, imagining that you are talking to an eager listener. Concentrate on the content of the tale, not the words. (It's fine if you have to borrow some words from the original teller; this is only practice.)

Then, afterward, take a few minutes to reflect: What did you notice as you did this practice?

2. Oral History

Oral history, as you probably know, is the recounting of real events by people who participated in them or witnessed them. Books like *Eyewitness to History* or Studs Terkel's many collections can provide you with material for stories. Try retelling a story from recorded oral history in your own words. If you prefer, take an historical event and invent a character to tell it. Talk the story onto the page to an imagined listener.

What did you notice in doing this? Take some time to reflect.

You can also, if you wish, be a collector of oral history. Do you have a relative or an acquaintance who has had an interesting life? Or perhaps you'd like to go to your local senior center and ask some of the people there to tell you stories. Most people are delighted to talk to an interested listener, and you will probably be amazed at the fascinating material you can collect.

You don't have to tape record or take notes (though you certainly can if you want to and your storyteller gives you permission). If you simply listen, and ask questions, and let the person's stories capture your attention, you will probably retain the material that is useful to you. Afterward, though, do take some time to jot down information in your notebook. (This activity is great practice to improve your listening skills and your memory.)

Now retell one of the stories in your own words, or take some materials from one or more stories and use them to put together a story. Try to tell this story as if you are telling it to someone in person.

What did you notice in doing these practices? Take some time to reflect.

3. Stories From the News

Many writers get ideas and materials for stories from news reports. Some writers love to read the obituaries for story material; others like to scan small, offbeat stories, or stories about crime.

Gather some newspapers and magazines and browse through them, looking for stories or bits of stories that grab your attention. Collect whatever material appeals to you, feeling free to choose bits and pieces from different stories. Let your imagination and your subconscious work on the material; play around with it. Then use this material (altered any way you choose) to tell a story, remembering to talk *to* your reader.

What did you notice in doing this? Take some time to reflect.

4. Gossip and Overheard Stories

Writers have always made use of stories other people tell, whether overheard or passed on as gossip. Henry James and F. Scott Fitzgerald, for instance, collected stories at dinner parties or from conversations with friends and made use of this material in their novels.

Spend some time in a place where you can eavesdrop on people's conversations and, as best you can without making yourself obnoxious, listen in. Take mental notes of anything that interests you and transfer those notes to your notebook later. (If you prefer, you can try taking notes as you listen, but make sure the people you are listening to don't catch you doing this!)

You can also try having a good gossip session with a friend, and then take some notes when you get home.

Look through the material you have collected, and select some details that speak to you. Try to put this material together into a story and tell it on the page to an imagined listener.

What do you notice in doing this practice?

5. PLACE AND THINGS

It's not only humans who have stories; other beings in the world—even places—can tell us stories, if we are willing to listen. Many folktales and myths, for instance, explain things about animals ("How Bear Got His Short Tail," for example) or plants (Native American stories about the Corn Maiden, for instance) or natural phenomena like thunder and lightning and rain.

Spend some time reading myths and folktales that explain things about a place or a natural phenomenon. Then brainstorm a list of things or places, or both, that appeal to you. Try making up a story about one or more of the things or places on your list, imitating the approach of the myths you have read. If you prefer, you could give your chosen place or thing a voice, and let it tell its own story.

Afterward take some time to reflect on what you noticed in doing these practices.

6. STORIES FROM WITHIN

So far we've been collecting material for stories from outside sources; naturally, we can also collect story material from inside ourselves, from our memories, our imaginations, or both.

You may find it helpful to begin by reading through the material you collected in earlier practices. Then, using the freewriting technique, write as many sentences as you can that begin with these words: *I want to tell a story about ...*

If you prefer, use the following questions to collect material for stories from inside yourself. In a relaxed way, write down your answers; try to keep your pen moving.

1. When you listen for stories you could tell, what people come to mind? Real people? People you've loved; people you've hated? Imaginary people? Whose voices do you hear?

2. What places come to mind? Real places? Imaginary places? A country/a landscape/a house/a street/a room?

3. What things come to mind? A favorite toy? Something you spend a lot of time with? Something in nature? An imaginary object?

4. What scenes or moments come to mind?

5. What ideas come to mind?

6. Are there any stories you've heard that you really love?

What did you notice in doing these two practices? If you feel moved to write a story now, go right ahead!

PRACTICE: Keeping an Ear Out For Stories

Professional writers never run out of ideas for stories because they have developed a kind of instinct for story. They don't write only about themselves—for, after all, how interesting is any one ordinary person's life? Instead they keep their attention on the world around them; they notice something, or they hear someone say something, and their story instinct says, *Hmmm ... there's a story in there.*

The more you can practice keeping an ear out for story material, whether it comes from oral tradition or oral history or people you encounter, the stronger your instinct for story will become. And if you make a habit of jotting down ideas or material for stories in your notebook, soon you will have a substantial store of "stuff" you can use in a story you want to write.

THE STORY-MAKING PROCESS

Sometimes stories are given to us whole, or almost entirely so. In this case, all we have to do is to retell the story in our own way. I think it's great practice in the craft of making stories to take a story that isn't "original"—a folk or fairy tale, for instance—and retell it. This doesn't have to be an elaborate piece of work or require weeks of effort. The more we retell established stories, the more practice we get in how stories are shaped and in talking directly to our readers.

Other times, we make stories out of material from different sources. Just like a cook, we combine various ingredients to make something new.

PRACTICE: Story Process

Brainstorm some ideas for stories, or look through your notebook to find ideas; pick one to play with. Now begin to collect material for this story: Start with internal collecting—all the details you remember or invent. Then (or at a later time, if you prefer) go back through this list twice: First mark the items you want to use when you tell your story, and write down any new ones that occur to you. The second time you read through your list, bring your curiosity to it and write down your questions. Then consider: Do you want to answer any of these questions before you tell your story? (If your chosen story is very simple, you may not have any questions you want to answer.) If you need to do some external collecting—observation or research—then do that.

Bring your imagination and your subconscious to your material: You may want to let your material simmer for a while before you write the story.

Now consider these questions:

Who is telling the story? That can be you or another real person or a character you invent.

To whom? You can pick a real person (a friend, perhaps, or one of your children), use an imaginary safe reader, or invent a character; in either case, though, use your imagination to picture this person clearly.

Why? What's the storyteller's purpose in telling this story to this particular person? What does she want to make happen in her listener?

Now, in your imagination, become the storyteller. Go back through the material you collected and select whatever seems useful to you to tell your story. (You do not have to keep to "facts" in this exercise; alter them and make up details however you like.) Add any new material that seems useful. If you want to make a little list of the order in which you want to use this material, go ahead. Then, keeping yourself in the role of the storyteller, imagine that you are with your chosen listener. Tell him or her the story, on the page, trying to keep your pen moving as much as you can.

What happened when you did this? What did you notice?

You might enjoy taking the same story and having someone else be the storyteller, or changing the audience, or both. Notice what happens when you do this. If you like playing around with telling a story from different viewpoints, take a look at the excellent anthology, *Points of View*, which illustrates, through published short stories, all the different things that can be done with point of view.

STORY AS HAPPENING

At its most basic, a story is a series of happenings. Jane Yolen, author of many books and collections of tales, has written, "And after all, it is not the expectation of a happy ending that carries us on. Rather it is the unraveling of the story itself; it is the traveling and not the destination."[13] One of the reasons I enjoy listening to baseball games on the radio is that the movement of a game is just like the movement of a story: There's a person in a situation—let's say a batter at the plate in the bottom of the ninth, with the game tied, a runner at third, and two out. Is the batter going to get a hit and be a hero, or will he strike out? Just as I keep listening to the game to find out what happens, so one of the main things that keeps readers reading a story is the pull of the question, "What will happen next?"

Traditional narratives such as folktales and fairy tales can give us excellent grounding in story movement. Such stories always begin with a character (a person, an animal, a supernatural being) in a particular situation: *Once upon a time there was a poor young man who left his parents' cottage to make his way in the world* ... And then it continues with happenings: Either something happens to the character, or the character makes something happen. Sleeping Beauty, for instance, is put under a spell (something happens to her); the Fool sets out to seek the hand of the princess, an action. That first happening sets the story in motion, and it rolls on from one happening to the next, until it comes to a stopping place.

Award-winning writer and teacher Ursula Le Guin reminds us that readers expect something to happen in a story: "Even if a narrative is just a trip down a supermarket aisle or some thoughts going on inside a head," she points out, "it should end up in a different place from where it started. That's what narrative does. It goes. It moves. Story is change."[14]

Story, then, is always movement, and letting our stories move is one more skill we can learn through practice.

PRACTICE: *Story Movement*

Choose a character and write down a simple story situation for him or her, one you take from your reading of stories or from your own invention. Use only a few sentences to sketch the situation. Now tell something that happens to the character, or something the character does to respond to the situation. Again, use only a few sentences. Now answer the question: *And then what happens ...?*

If you like, keep asking and answering that question until your story comes to a stop.

What did you notice in doing this?

STORY PLANNING

Some writers can't work without an outline. (I've read that Faulkner outlined his novels on the walls of his house.) Other writers—Stephen King, for instance—don't outline at all. King has written that he sits down to write a story with nothing more than a situation and some characters in mind and lets the story unfold from there. It may be that the trick here is not to decide whether you are a planner or not, but to have some planning tools available and be able to decide, at any given moment in your process of writing a story, whether you want to use them. There's no reason you have to plan out your entire story in advance, unless you want to, just as there's no reason you can't make use of an outline after you've already written part of the story.

To equip yourself to plan effectively, take a look at Jon Franklin's *Writing for Story*, a book for aspiring journalists that offers a detailed story planning method.

PRACTICE: If You Like to Plan ...

One way to define story is as a connected series of happenings. If you want to carefully plan out the happenings in a story, here's one way to do it:

1. Pick one of your story ideas. Then, keeping your pen moving as best you can, list all of the events in the story. Write a short

sentence for each one; use the present tense, for now. You don't have to put them in order yet, and don't worry about your word choice. Write each event on a new line. Skip a line between each event and the next. If you have a variety of ideas about which events should go into your story, try different versions.

2. Now read through your list of events and choose the ones you want to include. Do you have too many events? Too few?

3. Now put these events in an order that makes sense to you, and use your plan to write your story.

PRACTICE: Letting the Story Unfold

Here is an alternative to making a plan for your story:

1. Choose one or more characters and put them in a situation.

2. What happens next? A character makes a decision, takes an action—or some other outside event or force intervenes.

3. As a result, the character is in a new situation. How does he or she respond to that situation?

4. What happens next?

5. Continue this movement forward from situation to happening or response to new situation, and so on. Is the story finding its path? Where does it end?

What do you notice about writing a story in this way?

ORDERING FOR THE READER

Whether you plan a story in advance, or not, you will have to think about the *order* in which you want to present your material. When

How to Be a Writer

we collect, using our creative faculty, ideas and bits of information come to us at random; but when we give these ideas and bits of information to our readers, we *must* order them in such a way that they make sense to them. The appropriate ordering of our material is one of the main ways in which we make ourselves clear to others. Remember that the reader is not inside your head! When you tell your story, you may already know all of the things you are going to say; the reader does not. The reader can make sense of the things you tell him only one piece at a time, in whatever order you present them in.

Imagine that you have asked for directions in an unfamiliar place. The person giving them to you says, "Well, you go six blocks and then turn left, then take your first right, and—oh! I forgot to tell you to go straight through the light at the gas station." Now, listening to this, you are confused. All the pieces are there, but they are out of order; so you can't make sense of them. Exactly the same thing can happen when you write. Even if every piece is there—every image, every description, every idea—if they are out of order, your reader will have a difficult time making sense out of them.

You don't want to create difficulties for your reader, because then she might just stop reading and throw away your work. So you must be considerate toward your readers and not confuse them. You need to ask yourself, as you contemplate your material, *What do I need to give my reader first so he can make sense of what comes next? What do I give him second? Third?* The more experience you have had with writing *to* others, the easier it will become to decide how to order your material. It starts to become second nature to think, *Will my reader understand this if I put it here? Have I left out a step? How do I keep her from getting lost in this part?*

One of the things that makes ordering for the reader challenging—and fun—is that you can order not only so the reader will understand what you are saying, but also to create different effects in the reader at different times. Sometimes the genre you are working in will automatically define how you need to order material. For example, if you are writing about a murder, and the killer has been found, in a news report you will present that information in the first paragraph. But would you do that if you were writing a murder mystery? Of course not—all the suspense would be gone and no one would bother reading the rest of the book! You can think about how you want each bit of your material to affect your reader—to grab her interest, perhaps, or to keep her in suspense—and then consider where you should put it in your piece: *Should the scene with the monkey come before or after the love scene?* When you consider how to help your reader follow the happenings of your story, that gives you one way to make such choices. So does thinking about the effect you want each bit to have on your reader. You have to find a good balance between the two.

Naturally it takes a lot of practice to get good at this business of making things clear to readers and finding ways to order your material so it will move them as you intend. Study how writers you admire do this: When you're holding your breath in the middle of a murder mystery, see if you can note the place, and then come back later (after you've found out what happens) and figure out how the writer put things in an order that created suspense. Share your work in progress with readers and see if they can tell you how they are feeling as they make their way through your writing. Experiment with creating different effects by taking the same material and ordering it in various ways.

By the time you feel comfortable doing these things, you will have long ago lost any fear of readers that you might have had. Now you are beginning to understand the power writers can have which enables them to get their ideas and images into other people's minds and to make things happen inside them. Now you may begin to see that at a certain level writing involves encountering, wrestling with, and (with luck and diligence) solving various specific problems: *If I put the monkey scene first, then my readers might be laughing too hard to really experience the love scene. But if I put the love scene first, then the monkey scene seems too crass. I wonder if I need something in between* ... This is the kind of dialogue that writers have with themselves all the time. Identifying and solving problems is one of the main things that writers who want to communicate spend their time doing. Much of this problem-solving happens during the revision stage of the writing process. Although techniques of revision for imaginative genres are beyond the scope of this book, you may find useful some of the techniques offered in the chapter seventeen: "Getting It Written."

Struggling with specific problems is one of the main ways that you learn as a writer, and one of the main ways that you get better. Often people who want to write are surprised by how much there is to learn; I've had folks in my workshops look up in amazement from a practice we're doing and say, "I never realized that writing was so much *work!*" It's the willingness to learn, the willingness to do the work, that separates the real writer from the wannabe. But difficult and frustrating as finding solutions to writing problems may be, there's nothing like the satisfaction you feel when, after hours of trying one thing after another, you finally do discover the solution you need, when you can finally exclaim, *I did it! I made it work!*

CHAPTER 14

Voice

Voice, of course, has a strong connection with your imaginary reader.

—Joan Aiken

When you practice writing to, rather than for, readers, you will inevitably begin to develop your own individual voice on the page. And the more confidence you have in this voice, the easier it becomes to develop a piece of writing—knowing you have a voice you feel comfortable with enables you to discover more things to say. Voice is also an essential characteristic of all good writing, so let's examine it more closely.

Imagine that you are talking face-to-face with someone, gesturing with your hands, making eye contact and breaking it, emphasizing a word or phrase by putting more energy into it. Now imagine that your hands have been taken away, then your eyes, your face, your whole body. What is left to get across your meaning to the person you are talking to? Only your voice.

This imaginary scenario is your real situation when you write: For your voice on the page is the bridge—the only one you have—that carries meaning from your mind into the mind of another person, your reader. And it's only your writing voice that can move that person in the way you intend.

It's easy to recognize voice when we hear someone speak, but what is voice in writing? Most simply, voice on the page is the sound of a person speaking which, as we read, we can hear with our "inner ear." Every good writer has his or her own distinctive voice (or, sometimes, voices); we can often identify a particular writer just by the sound of her voice on the page.

One's writing voice is not necessarily the same as one's speaking voice: Whether we are writing a novel or a magazine article, it's unlikely that the voice we use will sound exactly like the way we speak. Nonetheless, there is something that is uniquely "us" in those words on the page. This matter of finding one's own voice is something that beginning writers often struggle with. Why is that?

THE TYRANNY OF VOICELESS WRITING

We live in an era when voiceless writing predominates. In the academy, in corporations, in governmental bureaucracies, keeping the sound of a live human being *out* of one's writing is the required norm. Just listen to this example:

> The ontological relativity advocated here is inseparable from an enunciative relativity. Knowledge of a Universe (in an astrophysical or axiological sense) is only possible through the mediation of autopoietic machines.[15]

And to this one:

> Our complex, metastatic, viral systems, condemned to the exponential dimension alone... to eccentricity and indefinite fractal scissiparity, can no longer come to an end.[16]

Such prose ignores the fundamental truth about the act of writing: It is a way for one human being to communicate with others. But many of us have no choice about writing like this: Our jobs or our schoolwork demand it. After year upon year of writing such voice-less prose, it's no wonder that many people feel they have no writing voice of their own. Even worse, when we must write for people who intimidate us, such as a particular professor or boss, we can feel that our own writing voice has been silenced forever.

HOW TO RECOVER YOUR VOICE

If you feel that you have lost your voice on the page—or never found it in the first place—don't despair. There are ways you can find or recover it. And it's actually much easier and safer to find your own voice in writing than in life, as long as you do it through practice writing. In life, once words are said, they are out there. But you can say anything you want to on paper, and no one will ever hear those words unless you choose to show them. That privacy gives you the freedom to be bold, to experiment, to play with different voices. If you don't like the sound of one voice, you can try another; you can let your voice change and develop over time. And it has been my experience that, in strengthening one's writing voice, one also can strengthen one's speaking voice.

These days many teachers of creative writing seem to believe that to find an individual voice on the page, a beginning writer must excavate his or her most personal (preferably traumatic) experiences and share them with readers. I don't agree: You can discover your voice in much less painful ways, and your writing voice does not *have* to be a confessional one. Consider the following approaches for discovering and training your voice:

1. Get comfortable with private writing. Some beginners (or those who have been wounded as writers) may find that to discover a natural writing voice they must, for a while, engage only in private writing. Such a writer may need to hear and feel comfortable with his writing voice for a while before attempting to use it in writing to others. If this is the case for you, then by all means, take all the time you need. There is no rush. You can find your writing voice, over time, by doing all of the practices in this book that help you develop your writer's powers. While you are finding the subjects you want to write about and discovering things to say about them, you will also be practicing using your voice on the page. And when you have things to say that you really want to share with others—*I want to tell you this! Listen to the cool things I've discovered!*—then you can practice using your voice to share them.

2. Develop confidence in your powers. Taking the time you need to develop your powers will give you confidence that you have things to say. Beginning or inexperienced writers often sound insecure on the page, like people who don't believe they have anything to say worth hearing: *er ... Excuse me ... I just thought that maybe ... um, perhaps ... oh well, never mind ...* Experienced writers, by contrast, are often (on the page) like people who have a lot of confidence in themselves: *Just listen to what I have to tell you!* The confident writer's voice is powerful and strong. (In writing, as in life, occasionally what sounds like confidence is merely bravado.)

There seems to be a popular assumption these days that the only way to get that kind of power into your voice is to talk about yourself and your own experiences; then your voice will be "authentic," and (therefore) your writing will be good. A writer's voice does have to have power—after all, that voice has to carry meaning from her mind into the minds of readers. But power doesn't necessarily come from authenticity; it comes from *authority*. A writer's voice needs to sound, not authentic, but *authoritative*: It needs to have a sound in it that indicates that the writer knows what she is talking about. And how do we get that sound into our writing voice? By getting to know our subjects as well as possible, and by being clear in what we have to say about them. Strengthen your writer's powers; collect and develop your material—these activities will bring the quality of authority to your writing voice.

When you have that authoritative quality in your writing voice, readers will trust you, because they will feel that you know what you are talking about. Even if you are writing fiction, readers still need to feel that you know your material—that you know the world and the characters you have invented.

3. Practice writing to readers. Since it can take some time to break lifelong habits of voiceless writing, it helps to do a lot of practice in reestablishing the natural relationship between writer and reader, as described in the previous chapters. Whether you share your words with live human beings or not, practicing writing *to* someone will naturally bring to your words the energy and aliveness of voice.

You can also have a good time playing around with using different voices on the page. Think about how we change voices in real life depending on whom we're talking to. If you are explaining to your five-year-old why he can't have more candy, you will probably use a different voice from the one you use to make a presentation to a client at work. The same thing can happen in writing. The voice a writer uses on the page is not always the same: It depends on what he's saying, on who his readers are, and on the effect he wants his words to have. A writer who wants primarily to make her readers laugh will use a different voice than if she is trying to inform them or make them think seriously about a subject. You can experiment with different voices by asking yourself these questions with a piece that you are working on: Who is speaking? To whom? For what purpose? Often a piece of writing won't come together until the author has found the right voice for it. Experiment with various purposes: Write to persuade readers to do something; write to inform; write to entertain. If you're feeling brave, read your practice writing to other people and find out whether you've achieved your intended effect.

PRACTICE: *Playing with Voice*

Pick a subject and collect some material. Then choose a specific reader or group of readers, real or imagined. Write to a five-year-old or to someone who's ninety-five. Write to mothers or to people who hate children. Write to people who know lots about your subject or to people who know nothing. Now write to your chosen audience in a voice that feels appropriate. Now keep the same subject, and write about it to a different audience. What happens to your voice?

4. Be considerate toward readers. There's a quality that all readers appreciate in a writer's voice. That quality is what I think of as considerateness: The writer remembers that the reader is not inside her head, and she takes the time to guide him carefully through what she is saying so he won't get lost or confused. When we read writing like this, we relax, recognizing that we won't have to work unnecessarily hard to understand it. If you remember that it's your job to make your writing clear and understandable to your readers, your voice on the page will have this quality of kindness.

5. Listen to your writing. To develop your voice, you also need to learn how to listen to your own writing: Reading one's words aloud is an essential writing practice. Many beginning writers find this difficult. But even though you may cringe at first when you hear your words (the way people often do when listening to the playback of their own recorded voices), persevere. Don't judge your voice, just listen to it: What do you notice? See if you can detach a little from the words you wrote and really hear what your voice is saying. Are you making sense? Is there a quality to this voice that you like? See whether you can find the specific words or sentences that have that quality; then try to write other things using that voice. Learn from yourself. Trust your writer's intuition.

Some people find it helpful to read their words into a tape recorder and then listen to the recording—or to have someone else read them aloud. However you do it, though, make hearing your writing out loud one of your regular practices. Doing this does more than let you hear your voice; it helps you hear the content of your writing as if you were a reader—which makes it much easier to revise.

6. Read for voice. You can also learn about voice from the writers you love. Read their words aloud and listen to each writer's voice. What characteristics does it have that you like? Do some experimenting and try to imitate that voice. Then try the same practice with another favorite writer.

Most of all, it is a writer's choice of words and her particular way of putting those words together that creates her distinctive voice on the page. Getting to know words and learning how to combine them is—naturally—central to becoming a writer; but the craft of using words is a big subject, and I decided that I could not do it justice in this book. So in the following chapter we'll take only a very brief detour into the world of words.

 ## HOW TO READ ALOUD WITH YOUR CONTENT-MIND

- Relax. If you tend to criticize your writing as you read it, try to let go of those critical voices in your mind. You are not going to judge your writing; you're just going to listen to it.

- As you read, slow down. Naturally, since this is your own writing, you're already familiar with the content of your piece, so it's easy to speed up as you read. But when you slow down, you can hear what you have said.

- Try not to focus on the words. Instead, listen to your writing with your content-mind. Simply notice what you are saying, how your voice is getting across your content. Let yourself notice, for example, whether there are places where the content is exactly what you want or whether there are places where you have left things out. Perhaps, too, you have repeated things that don't need to be repeated; perhaps there are other places where you need to repeat something: a gesture, a theme, a detail.

- If you like, imagine that you are someone else who is listening to your piece. Notice how this person responds to what you are saying with your voice.

CHAPTER 15

A Few Words on Words

The greatest possible merit of style is, of course, to make the words absolutely disappear into the thought.

—NATHANIEL HAWTHORNE

By now you may be wondering: *But what about words? Isn't writing really about words?* No. And, yes.

Naturally in order to write we need to use words, but those words must be communicating something—there needs to be some *content* behind them. The writer must have something to say. In my years as a teacher I've seen many pieces of writing that consisted only of empty words, connected to nothing real or fully imagined.

Even when a writer does have things to say, trying to figure out exactly what those things are and trying to communicate them clearly and powerfully *at the same time* (as in the one-step model of the writing process) will often prove difficult. As you've done various practices, you've seen that you can use writing to find your subjects and discover what you want to say about them without worrying about your words. When you focus your attention on developing your powers or developing your material for a particular piece of writing, and on using your voice to say those things to readers, the words you need will often come to you.

Over the years I've found that beginning or stuck writers often get so obsessed with finding the perfect words that they forget they need to be communicating something to their readers. *Just say it!* I tell them. *Tell me out loud what you are trying to say.* Most of the time I will receive, out loud, a far clearer recital of what the writer intends to say than anything that's on the page. *Great!* I say. *Now write down what you just said.* When you get stuck with a piece of writing, instead of fiddling with the words, try this: Ask yourself, *What am I trying to say?* and just talk your response onto the page.

At the same time, there's no doubt that finding exactly the right words can also help us clarify our ideas and images: In the process of trying to articulate them clearly, we discover what they are. It's also true that, while following the process approach and concentrating first on finding things to say and then on communicating them usually works very well, writing can also work the other way around: Fooling around with words can sometimes lead us to things we didn't know we wanted to say.

The "what-I'm-saying" and the words are really two sides of the writing endeavor, the yin and the yang. Writing is like a dance between content and words: Sometimes what-I-want-to-say leads, sometimes the words take over. The real art of writing is to manage a sustained balance between the two. But when we're learning, it can help to practice each one separately.

In the practices presented in this book, I have emphasized (some might say overemphasized) content because I feel strongly that, without interesting content, even the most technically accomplished writing is meaningless. Yet it's also true that we can read some writers, not so much for what they have to say, but for the way they say it. We read such writers for the sheer delight we take in their word artistry:

It was an empty, oyster-and-pearl afternoon. The water lipped at the sand and sorted the shingle and lapped around the rock where the girl was sitting.

—Kevin Crossley-Holland, "Sea-Woman" in *British Folktales*

Marley was dead: to begin with. There is no doubt whatever about that. The register of his burial was signed by the clergyman, the clerk, the undertaker, and the chief mourner. Scrooge signed it; and Scrooge's name was good upon 'Change, for anything he chose to put his hand to. Old Marley was as dead as a door-nail.

—Charles Dickens, *A Christmas Carol*

'Twas brillig, and the slithy toves
Did gyre and gimble in the wabe;
All mimsy were the borogoves,
And the mome raths outgrabe.

—Lewis Carroll, "Jabberwocky"

In a hole in the ground there lived a hobbit. Not a nasty, dirty, wet hole, filled with the ends of worms and an oozy smell, nor yet a dry, bare, sandy hole with nothing in it to sit down on or to eat: it was a hobbit-hole, and that means comfort.

—J.R.R. Tolkien, *The Hobbit*

For writing is indeed a matter of content; and, at the same time ... there are *words:* oh! glittering, tough, silverquick, moonslow, daring, fearsome, magical WORDS! Oh, yes—writing is indeed all about words.

And so as practicing writers we have another area to play and experiment in: the land of words. Perhaps this is the area where inexperienced writers feel the most insecure, where the thought, *I just don't have the talent,* is most often expressed. Yes, many writers we call "great" do indeed have a wonderful ability to use words, and perhaps we may never get to their level. But learning how to use words is learning the craft of writing, and I firmly believe that *anyone* who wants to can learn it. Because it's so widely assumed that the ability to use words well is a gift only a few possess, it's rare that the craft of writing is actually taught in schools. Not grammar, not spelling, not—heaven help us—the "five-paragraph theme," but the craft of putting words together in such a way that they essentially perform magic on the page: They transfer our ideas and imaginings into other people's heads as clearly as possible; they make things happen inside our readers.

This craft, like any craft, can be taught; and it can be learned. Such a deep craft it is, though, with so much to learn, that it helps, I think, to consider it separately from the material presented in this book. For it takes time and focused practice to train your craft-mind: to get to know words well, to learn how to put them together to create spells that will grab and hold your reader's attention, that will move her mind and take her imagination to the places you want it to go. When you have the opportunity to put your attention exclusively on words for a while, you can learn a lot about that aspect of writing, about technique, and then, when you want to write your stories or essays or poems, you'll have more skills available to you. (The companion book to this one, tentatively titled *Wordcraft*, will be a guide to the craft of making things with words, full of practices to help you learn that craft. In that book, I will invite you to devote all of your attention not to what you have to say, but to words themselves—their meanings, their histories, their music, their magic—so that you can learn how to use them well.)

Learning to write is, as I said at the beginning of this book, a lot like learning how to hit a baseball, or how to ride a bike. Writing, like these other activities, is a complex skill. So, just as when you're practicing hitting, you might put your attention for a while on keeping your eye on the ball, and then switch it to keeping your bat at a certain angle, and then later put it into following-through with your hips, so with writing, you can practice developing your powers, or writing to readers or finding your voice or using words, one at a time. Then, eventually—just as a beginning hitter learns to put all the pieces together into one fluid swing, or a beginning bicyclist stops having to switch her attention from the road to the pedals to the handlebars and the brake, and can just *ride*—so, with practice, all the pieces that make up the complicated and wonderful activity we call writing can come together. And then every once in a while, as your various writer's powers work together, and you find just the right words to say what you want to say, you can head straight down that steep hill, lift your hands off the handlebars, and call out: *Look, Ma! I'm writing!*

SECTION 4
required writing

CHAPTER 16

Do I Have to Write That?

If we taught children to walk the way we teach them to write, they'd never learn.

—Mark Twain

The difference between the writing my adult students are doing in noncredit creative writing workshops and writing done in school or at work is freedom: freedom to choose their subjects, freedom to use whichever powers they want that will help them come up with things to say, freedom to choose an audience, freedom to share or not share, as they like, freedom to take their time with a piece and let it develop at its own pace.

Writing in school doesn't usually provide us with this kind of freedom. We *have* to write those papers. We *have* to use only our intellect and no other writer's power. We *have* to write on subjects of the professor's choosing and in ways that he demands. We *have* to get those papers in by the deadline. We *have* to have our writing graded.

Writing at work often doesn't give us much freedom, either. We *have* to write the report the boss assigns. We *have* to meet her deadline. And often we will be evaluated, perhaps even financially rewarded, according to how well we do with these assignments.

So far in this book we've been exploring a way to build writing skills under conditions of complete freedom. But many people

who want to write also have writing projects they *must* get done, at work or in academic courses. (Some of you may not ever need to do required writing projects; in that case, feel free to skip this chapter and the next one.) So in this section I offer you some tools to get those required projects completed. Some of these tools will already be familiar to you, if you have been faithfully doing the practices from earlier chapters; in this section you'll learn how to apply those tools in new ways.

When we are faced with a writing task we *must* do, as opposed to one we choose, it's easy to feel resentful and to express that resentment through procrastination. But required writing projects can help us learn to write, or to write better; when approached in the right spirit, these projects can strengthen our skills in ways that we can then apply to writing we want to do. Before we can see the value of required writing, though, we may need to examine our feelings about it.

PRACTICE: How Do You Feel When You Have to Write Something?

You can answer this question in general, or you can think of a specific writing project you must produce. Freewrite for ten minutes, letting yourself explore your feelings about required writing: Do you feel resentful? Anxious? Angry? What is it about this project that makes you feel this way? What could you do to make it easier to get this project done?

After you've finished, read through what you've written and then ask yourself: What did I learn from doing this exercise?

One reason we can feel frustrated by required writing projects is that they seem to eat up so much time! In the next chapter, you'll learn a technique for getting something written with as little unnecessary effort as possible. You'll become familiar with the steps of the writing process, so you know how to take a piece of required writing from start to finish.

There's another way to make required writing tasks less burdensome: See them simply as opportunities for more writing practice.

REQUIRED WRITING AS A PRACTICE

Most people feel—or to have been taught—that there is an absolute difference between "creative writing" and "the other kind": Poems and stories and plays are "creative"; academic papers and business reports or memos are not; creative writers are one kind of being; all other writers are another. I consider this attitude an exceptionally damaging one, for not only does it lead to the assumption that only certain people have the necessary "creativity" to write poems or stories; it also keeps us from using our creativity when we do required writing, with the inevitable result that we are bored and our writing is boring.

It doesn't have to be this way!

The creative faculty, as you know by now, is tremendously adaptable; it's willing to give you ideas on any subject in which you have an interest. There is absolutely no reason, then, to keep yourself from using it when you have an assignment to do at work, or a paper to write for school. The same thing is true with the other writer's powers: While you may not be able to include in a business report details of color or taste you gathered during the practice of using your powers of observation, that practice will make you familiar with the value of collecting specific details—and a business report, to be well-written, depends on specifics, just like any other piece of writing. (In this case, those specifics will be specific pieces of information rather than sensory details.) In similar ways, your memory and expertise, your curiosity, even your imagination, can contribute to putting together a piece of required writing, especially during the collecting phase.

So I encourage you to see writing that you must do as another opportunity for exercising your powers—and, even more, to look for ways you can use these powers as you write business letters or memos or put together a paper for school.

PRACTICE: Use Your Powers in Required Writing

Use freewriting to think about this question: Are there any ways you can use your writer's powers in the projects you are required to do at work or in school? Once you've come up with some general ideas, see if you can make them more specific. Afterwards, read over what you have written and, if you like, make some notes to yourself about how you can approach your next required writing project.

HOW REQUIRED WRITING BUILDS YOUR SKILLS

At the same time, writing at work and, especially, in school, can give you excellent practice in using another writer's power, one we haven't yet spent time with: the intellect, the mental faculty that works with information and ideas. For some peculiar reason, unknown to me, the intellect and the creative faculty are often perceived as mutually exclusive: An academic paper can't be creative; a story or a poem has to *only* be "creative"—does that mean it can't have any thought put into it? I know that this attitude comes from the way we are usually taught (I mean, *not* taught) how to write—but it just doesn't make any sense to me. The creative faculty can collaborate with the intellect just as it can with any of the other powers. An academic paper can certainly be intellectually creative, and a piece of "creative writing" devoid of thought will probably also be devoid of meaning and interest. You may be surprised to discover the ways that your intellect, strengthened through use in required writing projects, can contribute to writing you have chosen to do, especially in helping you clarify what you want to say and in selecting things to help you communicate that meaning to your readers.

Writing skills really are transferable from one kind of writing project to another. Our writer's powers will serve us whether we are writing a short story or a report at work—though different kinds of writing may demand more use of one faculty than others. The important thing is to *notice* how we are using our powers, and to find new ways to practice using them, no matter what we write.

After all, the basic goal for any kind of writing is always the same: to communicate our meaning clearly to our intended readers, and to affect those readers as we intend. So the techniques of considering audience and purpose we began to explore in *Moving Toward Readers* are also essential when we write at work or in school. Every time we think about our readers or the effect we want to have on them, we are practicing these particular techniques. Required writing can give you lots of good practice in this area, and you can come back to your chosen writing with improved skill. Considering audience and purpose when you write a memo at work will help you do the same thing when you write a poem or a short story.

Then, too, a writing project is a writing project, whether it's a novel or a Ph.D. thesis or an annual report: The process of putting together a piece of writing designed for readers is, at its most basic, pretty much the same, regardless of genre. So when you practice taking a piece of required writing through the steps of the writing process as described in the following chapter, you will be learning things about that process which you can also apply to a poem or short story you're writing (with appropriate variations in the process depending on the genre you're working in).

In this *Required Writing* section, I have outlined the steps of the writing process so that you can learn how to get things written when you have to. The more you practice these steps, the more confidence you will have in your ability to complete a piece of writing to your (and your readers') satisfaction. You should then be able to get required writing done more efficiently, leaving you more time for the writing you want to do. Even more important, this increased confidence—just like the writing skills themselves—can be transferred to your own writing projects. And if all you've ever done is required writing, this confidence may embolden you to try something of your own. So I urge you to see required writing as simply more practice writing, which will, over time, make you into a better writer, no matter what kind of writing you are doing.

CHAPTER 17

Getting It Written

The key to confidence lies in preparation.
—Former Red Sox pitcher Dennis Eckersley

What makes required writing so hard? When I ask this question in my writing workshops at Harvard Divinity School, I receive a variety of answers: *I always put it off until the last minute. I have a hard time figuring out what I really want to say. I never know if I'm making sense to anyone else. I don't know how to organize. I'm terrible at spelling and grammar.*

One of the things that makes writing hard is that it is a complex activity. There are many things we must do in order to create a successful piece of writing—that is, a piece of writing which conveys to our readers what we want to say and which has the effect we intend: We have to get started, find a subject, find things to say about it, think about our audience and purpose, organize our material, make our meaning clear to our readers, get rid of mechanical errors, and so on. That's a lot! And what makes doing all of these things even harder is that most of us were never taught *how* to do them.

Most people were taught how to write according to the one-step model of the writing process: Get your meaning clear in your mind, make an outline, and then write—and your writing should come out perfectly the first time. If it doesn't ... well, either you can't write, or you're stupid—or possibly both.

204

While this one-step model can work well for some people, for most of us it doesn't work well at all. That's because it forces us to try to do all of the different things writing requires—coming up with things to say, and coming up with a way to say them—at the same time. It's as if we were baking a cake and had to measure flour, separate eggs, and bake the cake all at once. It's usually *much* easier to get things written when we replace the one-step model with an alternative model that sees writing as a *process,* as something that happens not all at once, but in logical steps. When you understand all the steps of the writing process, and when you know what you need to be doing at each step, then you will be able to get things written more efficiently and with considerably less stress and anxiety. This chapter will introduce you to this alternative model, often called the *writing process approach.* If you have done the exercises in earlier chapters, you will notice that in using this approach you will draw on the skills you have developed, and you will see how you can make use of these skills when you have a writing project you must get done.

Let's turn now to the process ...

GETTING IT WRITTEN: A STEP-BY-STEP GUIDE TO THE WRITING PROCESS

This new seven-step approach may take some getting used to, so be patient. Your old familiar way of getting things written—though it may cause you sleepless nights and knotted stomach muscles—has worked for you to some degree so far. You may find it difficult to abandon it for a new approach. Take it slow: Try this approach with one paper or memo, then another. Give yourself time to see how it works. And there may be some parts of it that work very well for you right now and others you need to give yourself more time to get used to. Remember that this book is giving you tools, not rules; use whichever ones you find helpful.

One easy way to understand the process of getting something written is to see it as having two main stages: content and communication. In other words, first you have to come up with things to say; then you have to communicate those things to your intended audience. One of the reasons the one-step approach to writing fails us is that it is extremely difficult to come up with things to say and communicate them well *at the same time*. So we need to learn how to do these things separately. With this in mind, consider the following seven crucial steps for a required writing project:

1. Define your project.

2. Plan your project.

3. Develop content.

4. Write a zero (discovery) draft, if you need to.

5. Consider audience and purpose.

6. Communicate.

7. Clarify.

If you have been regularly doing the basic freewriting practice, by now you will have discovered that it isn't all that difficult to get your thoughts on paper. You will have become comfortable using your creative faculty relatively unimpeded by your critical faculty. The more practice you have in doing this, the better; for it's the creative faculty that comes up with the content of your writing—and content is the most important part of required writing, whether it be academic or professional. We'll be using the freewriting technique throughout this chapter, so if you're not familiar with it, I recommend that you read chapter three before going further. Now, let's take a closer look at each one of these steps.

STEP 1: DEFINE YOUR PROJECT

Some writing tasks are simple: a memo telling coworkers about a meeting or a two-page paper based on our own experiences. But many writing tasks can feel completely overwhelming. This is especially true for academic research papers; because there's so much to learn, we can feel that a paper has no boundaries. But a paper, like anything else we may write, is simply a *project*, like planning a dinner party or knitting a sweater. Like any project, it has limits; for the success of your project, and the preservation of your sanity, you must know those limits.

Required writing is writing that someone else asks you to do; so before you begin, make absolutely *sure* that you understand your assignment. Usually you will be given at least some of the parameters for the project: how long it should be and when it is due. Often you are also given a subject to write about—the causes of World War II, for example, or the feasibility of putting in a new road. The most important thing your assignment should provide is what you are being asked to *do* in this piece of writing. Are you being asked to find an answer to a specific question? To analyze something? To explain something? Read the assignment directions over and over; put them into your own words; check with other students or coworkers. Make absolutely *sure* you know what you are being asked to do. If you write a paper on an assigned topic but don't do what you are being asked to do—if, for instance you simply summarize what an author has said rather than analyze it, as you were asked to do—then you will most likely not get a good grade.

Unfortunately, those who hand out writing assignments, be they tenured professors or supervisors, are not necessarily good communicators. Sometimes they do not make clear exactly what it is they want you to do. In that case, you must go and ask for clarification. There's absolutely no point in spending time trying to fulfill an assignment if you don't understand it. And since you can't read your professor's or your supervisor's mind, you have to go and speak to him or her. If you are a student and too afraid to go alone, see if you can get others in the class to go with you. If you are doing an assignment at work, try to formulate specific questions you can ask about both content—what kinds of things does your boss want to have in this report?—and, even more important, about purpose: What effect does she want this piece to have on its intended audience?

You also need to be sure you know what you are going to write about—the subject of your piece of writing. If you are being asked to choose your own subject, use nonstop writing to list every idea for a possible topic that comes into your mind. Don't censor anything. Keep your pen moving for at least five minutes. Then go back and look through your list and mark the subjects that look most interesting to you. (If you don't like anything you came up with, try this exercise again at another time.)

As you decide among your possible subjects, make sure the one you pick is workable. First, it should be a topic that you are interested in. Without that interest, it's difficult to muster the energy you'll need to research and write a paper. Second, your subject should be narrow enough so that you can cover it intelligently in the number of pages you have available. Often inexperienced writers choose topics that are much too broad. Fifteen pages may seem like a lot of pages to fill, but when you've become comfortable with the writing process, you'll find it easy to come up with things to say. Third, you must be able to find enough material on your subject during the time you have available. Fourth, and most important, your subject *must* fulfill the assignment.

Once you are clear in your mind about your subject and your assignment, take a few minutes to define your project, on paper, in your own words.

STEP 2: PLAN YOUR PROJECT

Like any other project, such as a wedding or a vacation trip, a writing project can be planned—that is, the process of making it happen can be broken down into parts, and those parts can be ordered; you can also estimate how long you think each part will take you. The main thing that will help you plan a writing project is learning how the writing process works. You have to know what you need to be doing at different stages in the process. Once you've gone through the process a few times, you will be familiar with each step and have a sense of how long it might take you. As you're developing your understanding of the writing process, give yourself extra time for each stage. (You can also do another kind of planning for a writing project: making a plan for the piece itself. We'll get to that later in this chapter on page 213.)

For now, to start planning your project, take a look at what you wrote when you defined it. If you like, rewrite those sentences to articulate your goal for your project—what you want to end up with. For instance, you might write: *GOAL: a ten-page double-spaced paper that analyzes the causes of World War II;* or *GOAL: a five-page report that explains why our company should or should not develop a new widget.*

Now list everything you have to do to meet your goal, all the activities or steps particular to this project. Try to be as specific as you can, but don't worry about the order of the items. If you get stuck, try to imagine working on your project: What will you be doing? Or look at each item on your list and ask yourself, *Can I break this task into smaller tasks?* For an academic paper, you might think of things like: *I need to find a paper topic and get it approved by the T.A. That means I need to spend some time freewriting about this class and what interests me in it.* For a project at work, you might come up with items like: *Get details from Susan about that meeting I missed. Find out from her whether anyone in one of our other offices has researched new widgets before.*

When you have gone as far as you can with this list, stop, take a break, and then come back to it. Now see if you can put the items in a common sense order: What will you need to do first, second, third, etc.? You may want to rewrite your list into a form you can use as a plan. If you can, estimate how much time you will need for each item, and write that down. Now, if you wish, set an actual deadline for each step, working backwards from the due date for your project. Remember to leave yourself a little extra time for things to go awry. Now put these dates into your date book, and, as best you can, hold to them as you work on your project.

MANAGING TIME

If you do a lot of required writing, you need to learn how to manage your writing time. If you take the process approach to several different pieces of writing, you will learn through experience what you need to do at each stage, and how long it is likely to take you for any particular project. The writing process approach can make you feel tremendously empowered as a writer, but you have to practice using it to get to that place.

One thing that you will learn is that most of your writing can be done in small chunks of time. If you have been hypnotized by the one-step model into believing that the only way you can get anything written is to take one long uninterrupted stretch of time to do it, I urge you to let go of that belief; all it does is encourage procrastination. Once you see that many parts of the process of doing a writing project can be done in short periods of time, then it's much easier to get something written. Another useful tool is your subconscious. Once you've become familiar with that faculty, it will help you work on your writing while you are doing other things, thereby making your process much more efficient.

How to Be a Writer

The most important thing you can do to make your writing process more efficient is to get started early. But what does "getting started" really mean?

Most people who put off getting started on writing projects are enslaved by the myth that they can't write anything until they've done all their reading and research. They are missing out on one of the most important truths about writing: It's not just a way to express things you already know, it's one of the most valuable tools you can find to help you *learn* and to help you discover what you want to say.

So getting started early doesn't mean writing a draft of your paper or report. It means moving on to the next step in the writing process: developing content.

STEP 3: DEVELOP CONTENT

As soon as you have defined your project, you can use writing as a tool to help you discover your content. First, you need to collect material; then you have to engage with that material and decide what you're going to use. The best place to begin collecting is through *internal collecting*. (If you've read the earlier chapters of this book, you already know how to do both internal and external collecting. Here we'll be applying these same techniques to required writing projects.)

INTERNAL COLLECTING

As you may recall from chapter three, internal collecting is simple: You look inside yourself to find out what you already know about your subject and what you need to find out. Here is a quick review of four of the best tools to help you do that.

Focused Freewriting

Bring your subject to mind, and then, using focused freewriting (keep the pen moving while keeping your attention on your subject), bring out from inside yourself anything you can come up with that has anything at all to do with your subject, and write it down. What do you know already about this subject? What information do you have? What do you think about it? Why are you interested in it? What are your expectations about what you will discover when you do some research? What questions do you have about your subject? What experiences have you had that make you want to write about it? Don't censor yourself: If, for whatever reason, you find yourself remembering your third-grade teacher as you write about the causes of the French Revolution, go ahead and put that down. You are not creating text here, so don't bother thinking about organization or spelling or anything except your subject; you are just collecting, from within, any material that you already have that you might be able to use.

Do this exercise for at least ten minutes.

Listing

Instead of freewriting sentences across the page, you can take the nonstop technique and use it to simply list all the things that occur to you as you do internal collecting on your topic. You don't have to order these items; just keep the pen moving. But do put each item on a new line—whether it's a single word or a complete thought.

Internal collecting is a great place to begin a writing project because it helps you see what you have and what you need. You may discover that you know more than you thought you did about your subject. You may discover that all you have are questions. Questions are a great starting place.

What happens during these collecting practices depends on how much you already know about your topic. If you know a lot, go on to the next practices. If you feel you need to learn more about your subject, skip to external collecting and return to mapping and interacting later.

Mapping

Another good collecting technique requires a fresh sheet of paper. Draw a small circle in the center of the page, and put your subject inside it. Then branch out single lines from that center circle, and on each line, as you collect, write down a new item. Use the material you collected during the focused freewriting and listing practices, as well as anything new that comes to you. So, on one line you might put a word or a phrase; on another line you might write down, in abbreviated form, an entire idea or piece of information. Then, as new things occur to you that seem to connect to things you've written down already, draw new branches that extend out from the ones on the page, and write down your new thoughts on those branches. Keep branching out as far as you can, and let yourself be intuitive as you do. Don't waste any energy wondering if you have "correctly" connected one branch to another; you can always fix it later. Try to keep your pen moving.

Mapping is particularly helpful because it enables you to get a picture of your entire project. This can help you see whether your subject is too big and needs to be more narrowly focused. It can also help you see its different parts and how they might connect. Sometimes, for a piece that is not terribly complex, a map or a list can, when you go back to it, give you a tentative order for the different parts of your piece.

Interacting

Read through everything you collected in whichever of the above internal collecting practices you chose to do. Read in a benign spirit—you do not have text here, so there's no point in correcting anything. Rather, pay attention to two things: First, mark anything that stands out for you—a word, a question, an idea, something that might become an idea. Second, interact with your words on the page by writing down any new ideas or questions that occur to

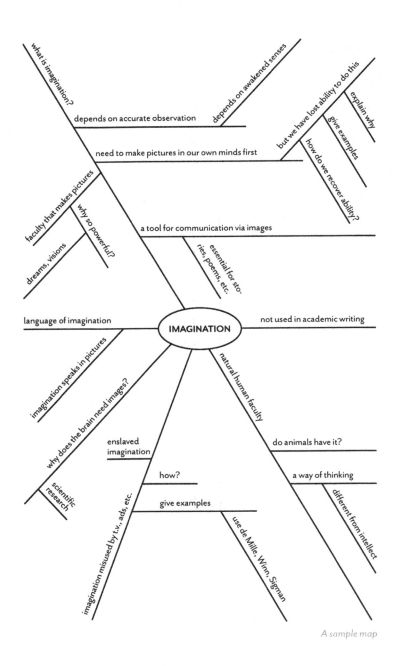

A sample map

How to Be a Writer

you. You can do this in the margins or on another sheet of paper. When you've read through everything, take whatever time you need to write down anything else that occurs to you.[17]

This practice of interacting is absolutely crucial, for it's in this practice that you have the conversations with yourself that enable you to develop the content of your project. It also helps you manage your project by showing you how it stands at present. When you are finished interacting with what you have written, take a moment to write down the answer to this question: *What do I need to do next with this project?*

You can use these four practices to get you started on any piece of required writing. For short, simple pieces, where you already know what you want to say, once may be enough. From this point in the process you can jump right to putting together a zero draft, or, if you prefer, to considering your audience and purpose and writing an assertion draft. (See later in the chapter for an explanation of these activities.)

But perhaps your answer to the question "What do I need to do next?" is: *I don't know enough to move forward with this piece. I need to learn more about my subject.* Then it's time to turn to the other collecting practice: external collecting.

EXTERNAL COLLECTING

Beginning a writing project with internal collecting is helpful because this activity enables you to see what you already know about your subject and where the gaps are—what you need to find out. It can also wake up your curiosity and get you excited about learning more about your subject. And coming up with your own questions—the things you want to know—can guide your research and help you use your time efficiently.

Being aware of your ignorance of a subject can be daunting, but remember that you don't have to learn everything about the subject in order to write a single paper. You might want to look again at your goal, and to consider exactly what you need to learn in order to achieve that goal. At the same time, it's very often the case that in order to create a good piece of writing, you will need to learn a lot about your subject—background knowledge—that you don't actually use in your piece. It can be frustrating to have collected a lot of information that you can't include in your project; remind yourself that you have learned something, and that what you have learned will make itself apparent. You may also want to keep a file dedicated to information you collect that you can't use; you'll be honoring your work and saving material that may prove to contain the seeds of future writing projects.

As we discussed in chapter three, external collecting—or research—can be undertaken as drudgery, or it can be done in a spirit of adventure. What will you find as you explore your subject beyond what you already know? How will you do your research? In the library? Online? Through interviews with experts? If you need help getting started, a good research librarian can help.

The most important thing to remember when you are doing external collecting is that you need to put time and energy into letting the material you collect become a part of you. If rule number one for required writing is *Know your assignment,* then rule number two is *Know your material.* My experience has taught me that many people have trouble writing academic papers, or doing complex writing projects at work, not so much because they can't put words together, but because they haven't given themselves enough time for mastering their material. So when the project is due and they sit down to write, they get paralyzed because they don't know their subject well enough to say anything intelligent about it. So it's essential to give yourself time not only to collect material, but to engage with it.

Academic papers (and many kinds of professional writing) demand the skilled use of a writer's power very different from the ones explored elsewhere in this book: the intellect, or the ability to understand and deal with ideas and information. It is this faculty that we need to use when we engage with the material we collect. Writing academic papers (or doing professional writing) typically involves coming up with an opinion or an idea about a subject and providing the evidence to support it. This practice helps train and strengthen your intellect. At its best, academic education trains us to think clearly and logically. Many people find this boring; they can't see its usefulness. And it's true that many academic assignments seem designed to doom student writers to boredom and frustration. But a well-developed (not overdeveloped) intellect is a pretty useful faculty to have. Life is full of situations where we have to make choices: what to do with an aging parent, for instance, or how to educate our children. Being able to collect relevant information, assess it, and think out our choices is a very useful skill. So, as you do the following practices, you will be developing your intellect as well as your writing ability. These practices use writing as a tool for learning, for making yourself knowledgeable about your subject. This writing is private writing; you don't have to show it to anyone. So you don't need to worry about the words you use or about spelling and grammar; instead, see if you can concentrate on making sense of the information and ideas you are collecting through research, and on developing your own ideas about your subject.

Engage with material

When you read a book or an article for a writing project, perhaps you take notes or underline passages you think are important. Such techniques, while they have their uses, don't really help you learn the material. That's because you can do them with about one-tenth of your attention, so you don't really take much in. So later on, when you want to use this material to write a paper, you get stuck. To help you assimilate material, try this: Read an article, or a chapter of a book, and then do some freewriting. Your freewriting should have two separate parts: In the first part, write down the important information you have gotten from this chapter, or what the writer is saying. Write down what you have understood clearly; write down what you have not understood. Write down your questions. In the second part, write down your intellectual reactions to what the writer said: What do you think of her ideas? Do you agree? Disagree? (You can write down your emotional reactions, too; they may help you find your ideas.) Repeat this practice with each chapter or section you need to read.

It's crucial to keep the two parts of this freewriting exercise separate, because one of the things that can be hard to learn is how to distinguish between what someone is actually saying and our responses to those ideas. It's easy to just react to someone's words; we do that all the time in life. But have we really heard what the other person was saying? Have we really *understood* her words? You may have had the experience of arguing with someone for a long time, and then finally realizing, "Oh, *that's* what you mean!"

Academic writing—as well as good writing at work—demands that our opinions about a subject be based on a solid understanding of that subject. Professors are usually looking for two main things in an academic paper. First, they want you to demonstrate your understanding of the subject. Second, they want to know what *you* think about some aspect of the subject, and they want to see that your ideas are grounded in an accurate understanding of the material. The more you practice responding to your reading in the way described above, the more you will train your intellect to engage in what is essentially a kind of silent conversation with the author. In this conversation you will both listen to the author and try your best to understand what she is saying (and if you don't understand, you can go back and read again, or seek clarification from fellow students or your professor), and you will begin to develop your own ideas.

Please notice that in doing this practice you will be writing a lot! So, as you learn, you will start becoming more comfortable just putting words on the page. You'll also be developing your creative faculty and discovering that, in combination with your intellect, it can often come up with good ideas. Remember that this writing is for no one's eyes but yours, so don't worry about word choice or mechanics. At this stage of the process you are not using writing to communicate; you're using it as a tool to help you learn. You are learning how to think on the page.

Engaging with a text in writing helps you make sense of the material and develop your own ideas much more easily and effectively than thinking by itself does. And, even better, when you think on the page about your reading, you are collecting material that you might be able to use in a paper. This doesn't mean that you will use every word you wrote; far from it. But you will have ideas on the page that you can come back to and develop.

If you are doing a project that requires research, you will soon find that you are collecting lots of material and have lots of pages written in response to that material. You will be able to work more effectively if you create a special place to put all this stuff—a notebook, a file folder or folders, folders on your hard drive. You may also want to carry around a small notebook to capture those ideas that appear at odd times when you are away from your desk.

Reflect

Another practice that can help you learn your subject and develop your ideas is to do focused freewriting periodically as you work on your project. Take ten minutes now and then to write about what you have learned and what you're thinking about it all. Keep the pen moving. This practice helps engage your creative faculty with your subject; you may be surprised by what good ideas it comes up with. Date this freewriting and put it into your file folder for your project.

As you reflect, use ordinary language. For many people, the language of an academic discipline feels like a foreign language; and it's very difficult to think well in a language you aren't comfortable with. So, for now, when you're still doing private writing on your project, use whatever language helps you generate and develop your ideas. Later on in the process you can, if necessary, translate your words into the language of a particular academic field or profession.

Use your subconscious

It's important to leave time in your plan for the subconscious to work on your material. You can use your writing time much more effectively when you make use of the power of the subconscious. (See chapter eight for details on how to use this power.)

If you do these "writing to learn" practices frequently, soon your file folder may start to bulge alarmingly. Add this next practice to your repertoire:

Interact

Read through all the writing you have done so far and do two things: Mark anything that stands out for you, and write down any new ideas or questions that occur to you. It's essential not to fix or edit your writing as you do this; the previous practices are not designed to give you text—they are designed to help you come up with and develop *ideas*. At this stage of the process it doesn't matter what words you use to express your ideas, only that you have some ideas. In fact, a crucial skill for academic and professional writing is to be able to look *through* your words to the ideas that are behind them or to the ideas that are trying to emerge.

Doing this interacting practice frequently, though it might seem like a lot of work, will actually save you time in the end, because it really does help you learn your material. It can also help keep you on track with your project, in two ways. After you've read through and interacted with what you have written, write down and complete this sentence: *What I'm really trying to say here is...* At this point in your learning you may not know what you want to say; that's okay—do your best to complete the sentence anyway. This little practice is not a test; it's a way for you to keep focused on an essential part of the writing process—that your paper will need to make a point. (More on this shortly.) When you do a lot of collecting and reflecting on your subject, you may get lost in all the possible directions your project could go; when you keep coming back to that question, *What am I trying to say here?*, you are more likely to stay on track. Don't be dismayed if your answer changes over time; that's actually a good sign—it means you are learning.

You can help keep your project on track in another way as well. When you've finished interacting, take a moment to answer this question: *What do I need to do next with this project?*

Keep track of your progress—of where you are in the process of doing a writing project—the same way you would track any other project. Keep asking yourself: *What do I need to do next?* Write down your answers. Leave yourself notes about what to do next so you can pick up on another day without wasting time. And don't forget to look back periodically at the assignment or your goal to make sure you haven't drifted away from what you are being asked to do.

At this point you may be thinking, *But I don't have time to do all this writing!* Perhaps you don't need to: short, simple pieces of required writing—a memo, for instance—may require nothing more than a few minutes to make a list of all the things you want to include in your draft. But, as I said earlier, if you have a more complicated piece to write—especially something that requires a lot of research or other learning—then if you don't take the time to collect and learn, you'll undoubtedly be sorry. When you must sit down to write the paper, you will likely discover that you are unprepared.

Besides, doing this kind of engaging with a text or with research material doesn't take that much time: All you need is ten or fifteen minutes for any one of the practices. And the benefits will amaze you. For one thing, you will really integrate what you are reading in a way that is very hard to do if you are just taking notes. What you learn will become a part of you—and that, after all, is a big piece of what real learning is all about. You will also begin to develop your own ideas about the subjects you are studying; as you think on paper about your material, as you ask questions of it, you will exercise and strengthen your intellect. And the more you practice using this faculty the more confident you will become in your ability to have and develop your own ideas.

In addition to all these benefits, these practices will actually save you time. As you collect and interact with what you have collected, and reflect on it, you will gather a big pile of information and ideas that you will be able to use in your paper. Naturally you won't use everything; your ideas will develop and change as you engage with your subject. And it's important to remember that you may end up using very few of your exact words from your practices. That's just fine. One of the reasons the writing process approach works so well is that it enables you to concentrate on one step of the process at a time: First you put all your energy into having and developing things to say; then you put all your energy into finding effective ways to say those things. If you have taken the time to use these practices for your project, you'll have a file folder full of the material you need to take your project to the next stage of the process: the zero draft.

STEP 4: WRITE A ZERO DRAFT

At a certain point in your process of collecting material and engaging with it, you will feel that you have enough material—or you will feel that you have so much that you're getting overwhelmed. This is a good time to put together a zero draft. This kind of draft gives you a way to see what you have and what you might still need. It's also a way for you to make choices about what to include and what to leave out.

A zero draft is a draft that comes before your first draft: It consists of everything you think you want to include in your piece written down on the page, somewhere, in a single document.

During the collecting and engaging-with-material practices, you have given your creative faculty a lot of freedom to help you come up with things you might say in your piece. Now it's time to bring in the critical faculty, not to judge what you have, but to help you *select* from everything you have collected the things you can actually use.

How will you make those choices? Go back to your assignment (or your goal statement) and review it; anything you choose to include *must* help your piece fulfill the assignment. You can also use a consideration of your audience and purpose to help you make choices. Most of all, you choose material that will help you get across your point.

WHAT'S THE POINT?

During this process of choosing your content, it's important to remember that, in most academic and professional writing, what you ultimately want to come up with is a point that is well supported by evidence. It really isn't enough to say lots of different things about your subject; you have to make a point. When I was teaching undergraduates, sometimes they would demand, "Well, *why* does a piece of writing have to have a point?" And I would say, "Because otherwise no one is going to want to read it." Imagine that you are talking to someone who is droning on and on, giving you lots of different pieces of information and ideas about a particular subject. After a while, you are going to be thinking, *Why are you telling me all of this stuff? What's your point?* This is how your reader will feel if your piece of writing has no point.

Academics like to call the point of a piece of writing its "thesis statement." Most students know that an academic paper has to have such a statement, but often they don't have the faintest idea how to find one. They seem to imagine that there is, somewhere out in the world, a particular tree that has thesis statements hanging all over it, and all they have to do is find the tree and pluck the particular statement that will suit their needs.

You can find a thesis statement—or, to use the term I prefer, the point you want to make—*only* through the work of engaging with texts or research materials. You can't possibly have a point to make in advance of doing this work; you have to go through the process of *discovering* it as you think and write about what you are learning. Putting together a zero draft is the next step in the process of discovering exactly what you want to say.

Imagine that you are going on a trip, and in preparation you have taken out of your closet every piece of clothing and pair of shoes that you might possibly wear; you have, in a sense, done a lot of collecting. Now you have to be realistic about how much of this stuff you will actually wear and can carry: You have to *select* from everything you've collected what you can actually use on this particular trip. This process of selection is a lot like putting together a zero draft.

When you pack for your trip, you may really want to bring that new red hat; but it doesn't go with any of the clothes you need. So you leave it behind. In a similar way, when you put together your zero draft, you're going to have to let go of things you have collected—fascinating bits of research or great ideas—that you can't use for this particular project. You may want to create a special folder to keep all this material. Once you make another place for it, you won't mind so much that you must take it out of this project.

You can put together your zero draft in various ways. If you are working at a computer, you can simply cut and paste from the documents where you have collected and reflected into a new document called "zero draft." You can also do this cutting-and-pasting by hand. If you prefer, you can read through everything you've collected, make a list of the different things you want to include, then put your notes aside and write a draft. Or you can use some combination of these approaches.

You don't need to order things as you put together your zero draft; the main purpose of the zero draft is to help you see what you already have and what you still might need. However, it may help you to gather into the same place in the draft different bits of material that seem to go together. Perhaps you want to create different sections into each of which you can put everything that seems to go together. Then perhaps you can create a tentative order for these sections. Making a map is also helpful.

Putting together a zero draft is a practice that will help you discover what you want to say. For that to happen, though, you must keep engaging with your material and asking yourself, *What am I trying to say?* How long this will take depends on how complex your project is and how much work you've already done. No one will see this draft but you, so don't spend any time agonizing about word choice. Keep your attention fixed on your ideas. You might find it helpful to ask yourself, out loud, *What am I trying to say here?* and then to write down what you just said. You may find it helpful to rewrite certain sections to make them clearer.

When you finish putting together your zero draft, print it out and read through it. Is it starting to make sense? Do you feel comfortable with the choices you've made about what to keep and what to leave out? Write down your answers to the questions: *What am I trying to say?* and *What do I need to do next with this project?* You may want to take a break now, to let your subconscious also work on these questions—go for a walk or take a rest. You may find that your subconscious gives you some very helpful answers.

Your answers to the questions will tell you what you need to do next: gather more information, do more thinking and writing about what you want to say, expand or rewrite your zero draft ...or take the next step in the process. If you feel that your zero draft contains everything you need to get your point across and that you have a clear idea of what that point is, then you're ready to think about your audience and your purpose.

STEP 5: CONSIDER AUDIENCE AND PURPOSE

One way to think about required writing is that it is writing we *know* someone else (usually the person who gave us the assignment and possibly others as well) is going to read. Required writing is inevitably public, not private, writing.

How we consider our audience and our purpose for a piece of writing can be a complex matter. (We discussed it in the section *Moving Toward Readers.*) Here, let's try to keep it simple. The key thing to remember is that a piece of writing is supposed to communicate something, to get whatever you have to say from your mind into the minds of others. But you have a choice about when to start thinking about those other people. Or rather, you have a choice *if you start early enough*. If you are working against a deadline, then you don't have a choice: You *have* to be thinking about your audience. Some people like this kind of pressure and swear they do their best work when subjected to it. If you're one of those people, then you know how to get work done under those conditions. But if you'd rather have more choice, and you're willing to get started on your writing projects earlier, as described in the preceding sections, then you do have a choice about when to consider your readers.

If you want to, you can bring your readers into your writing process right from the beginning. Why would you want to do this? Because sometimes thinking about your readers can help you come up with things to say. For instance, if you're putting together that proposal for the new widget, you might say to yourself something like: *Joe's going to want to hear about how much making a new widget will cost. I'd better include everything I can find about that.* When my Divinity School students have sermons to write for a congregation they know well, they often find it helpful to think about particular people in that group and their needs; doing so helps them come up with things to say.

Thinking about your purpose—the effect you want your piece to have on your readers—can also sometimes give you ideas for things to include: If you're writing a fund-raising letter, for instance, you'll need to think about the things you could say to your readers that will make them reach for their checkbooks. Or, if you're writing a paper and happen to know your professor's opinions on the topic, you may choose to highlight those in an attempt to get an A.

If you want to take the time to consider your audience and purpose in detail, here are some questions to help you do that. Write down the answers to the following questions:

- Who are you writing for? Give as much detail as you can about your readers.

- What do they know about your subject?

- What might they need or want to know about your subject?

- What might some of their questions be?

- What do you need to include in this piece of writing to answer these questions/give them what they need?

But some of the time—and, for academic papers, most of the time—thinking about your readers at the start of a writing project doesn't work at all. In fact, it may be that it's your fear of those very readers that is keeping you from getting started. If you find yourself procrastinating on a particular writing assignment, ask yourself how your reader makes you feel; if your answer is "scared" or "anxious" or "intimidated," then you know that you need to keep your reader out of your writing process until you absolutely have to bring him in. You must take this route, because if you don't your fear of your reader will keep you from being able to concentrate on having and developing your ideas. So, if you find yourself in this place with a particular writing project, it's especially important to start early so that you have the time to forget about your reader while you're developing the content of your paper; then, near the end, when you feel confident in what you are saying, you can consider that reader. Chances are, at that point, he will feel much less intimidating.

At the same time, it's crucial that you not forget that you *are* writing for someone else—someone who is not you. No matter who your reader is, be it your best friend or the president of your company, that person cannot possibly be inside your head. Even a professor, who may know more about your subject than you'll ever know, cannot know what *you* have to say about it. So coming up with things to say is only half the work; you also have to communicate those things, to transfer them from your mind to the mind of your reader. When you have a piece of writing that only you can understand—and in my years of teaching I've attempted to make my way through quite a number of such pieces—you do not have a successful piece of writing. You may have come up with good things to say, but you haven't *communicated* them. Think about what it's like to read such incomprehensible stuff—it makes you mad, doesn't it? Well, that's just how your readers will feel if *your* writing is impossible to understand. Outside of the academy, they won't bother to read it. Inside, while a professor will pick her way through such writing because she has to, she will probably give it a low grade—not because she didn't agree with you, but because she didn't understand what you were trying to say.

To avoid such a fate, here's a technique you can use at any time during the process of developing your ideas: *Write to a safe audience.* This extremely useful technique will teach you how to make yourself clear to others on paper. The technique is simple: Invent an audience you feel comfortable writing to—a friend, a coworker, a pet—and, then freewrite what you want to say while imagining that you are talking to this person on the page. Assume that this safe audience is interested in your thoughts, and that he will make no judgments on your words: He just wants to know what you have to say. Use your ordinary voice as you write, just as if you were having a conversation. (For more details on how to write to a safe audience, see chapter twelve.)

This technique of writing to a safe audience can really help you come up with and clarify your ideas; it can also be used, if you wish, in the next step of the process.

STEP 6: COMMUNICATE

Now that you've come up with what you want to say, it's time to communicate. It's time to write an assertion draft.

Another draft? I hear you say. *Are you kidding?*

Nope.

You may not have needed to write a zero (discovery) draft. With a simple piece of writing, you can certainly move right from collecting to an assertion draft. But if your project is complicated or requires a lot of learning, you may be doing yourself a disservice not to put together a zero draft and then do an assertion draft. What's the difference between the two, anyway?

With a zero draft, you can, if you need to, keep ignoring your reader for the time being and just concentrate on discovering what you have to say. For many people, for many projects (especially academic papers), this is a necessary step. It enables them to do one thing at a time—to come up with things to say—rather than trying to do that *and* communicate to their intended audience at the same time. For most people this one-step-at-a-time approach enables them to come up with better ideas.

With an assertion draft, you need to bring in an audience and, since you now know what you want to say, concentrate your attention on *communicating* your ideas to them. When you imagine a real person listening to you speak, that often encourages you to explain yourself clearly and not leave things out, as you might if you were just writing for yourself. It also helps you use your real voice on the page and get the energy of a speaking voice into your written words. While the zero draft and whatever revisions you may make to it enable you to get what you want to say clear to yourself, the assertion draft forces you to make that meaning clear to others. (Sometimes "talking" to another person on the page helps you make what you have to say clearer to yourself as well, just as in actual conversation.)

The other important difference between the zero draft and the assertion draft is that the former is a discovery draft. That means that as you put it together, cutting and pasting and writing new passages, you are finding out what you want to say. Sometimes, especially with an academic paper, you don't discover your main idea until right at the end of your zero draft. It's a great feeling when that happens, and you may be tempted just to polish up that zero draft and hand it in. But, before you do, consider this: If you ask a reader to read a discovery draft, you are asking him to accompany you on your process of discovery—that is, he won't find out what your point is until he gets to the end of your piece. In the work world, building a piece of writing step-by-step until it gets to the main point can sometimes work—especially when the writing is merely a guide for an oral presentation. But that's not usually the way academic papers are organized; in this particular kind of writing, the reader expects to get the main point—or the *assertion*—right at the beginning, usually at the end of the introduction. Then the rest of the paper is expected to support that point.

To assert means to state with confidence or force; that confidence comes when you have spent enough time engaging with your material that you know you have the evidence to support your assertion. If, for instance, you have decided that your company should not devote resources to making a new widget, you must be able to support that point: Perhaps the widgets are too expensive to make, or perhaps a competitor has a new widget on the drawing table already. If your point is that author A has a better understanding of *Beowulf* than author B, you have to support that point with examples from the writings of both authors and the poem itself. Sometimes students ask me, "Where do I get my evidence?" You get it from the work you did learning your subject: evidence is all the material—the information and ideas you collected as you read and did research—that led you to your point.

ORDER YOUR MATERIAL

Crucial to successful communication between you and your reader is the *order* in which you present your ideas and your evidence. That's because the order in which we receive verbal information has a lot to do with how well we can process it. So, in an assertion draft, you need to consider how to order your material so your reader can understand it easily. To do this kind of ordering, however, you need to be able to see that what you have in your zero draft is lots of chunks of material: Pieces of information, anecdotes, quotations from authorities, ideas, and so on. I've found that many people have difficulty seeing their material in this way; they seem to feel that, once they have written a draft, they have created a kind of monolithic entity, like a huge rock; and they are afraid to change anything because then the whole thing will crumble into dust. If this is the case for you, practice looking at your writing and trying to identify its pieces; for academic writing, identifying the different parts of a complex main point is a particularly helpful practice. And for most pieces of academic or professional writing, you need to distinguish between the points you are making and the evidence—the information, statistics, examples, anecdotes, and so on—that support those points.

When you order your material for a reader, you can consider your real reader, if she doesn't intimidate you, or a safe reader; or you can simply imagine someone who isn't you. (If you are writing for a professor, it's crucial to remember that, even though she may be an expert on your subject, she has no idea what *you* are going to say about it. In this regard, she is just another reader—who is not inside your head.) I like to think of my reader's mind as if it were an empty lot—which, in relation to an unfamiliar piece of writing, it is—and the pieces of my material as bricks made out of information and ideas. My job as a writer is to take those bricks, one at a time, and put them into that empty lot so that they fit together and create a nice, solid structure of meaning for my reader to spend some time in. As you plan the order for your piece of writing, keep asking yourself, *What does my reader need to know now? What comes first, second, third...?* In your discovery draft the order is determined by your process of discovery; essentially you are ordering for yourself. In your assertion draft, you must order for your reader.

How you make your plan for your assertion draft depends on how complicated your project is. Perhaps all you need is a little list. Perhaps you want to make a map. Perhaps you want to reorganize your zero draft by cutting and pasting into a new document. Perhaps you want to try different orders, using these techniques, to see what looks best. However you choose to create your plan, remember to think about the needs of your reader. Try, as you order your material, to anticipate your reader's probable questions and make sure you answer them.

If you want to, you can also play around with ordering your material to create certain effects on your reader as well as to communicate your meaning. Sometimes it makes no difference to meaning how the different things a writer has to say are ordered, but a particular order—perhaps withholding a crucial piece of information to keep the reader's interest—makes the writing more powerful. It's much more likely that you will find opportunities for doing this kind of thing with professional writing than with academic papers. (For instance, if you are writing a termination letter to an employee, you will probably want to soften the blow by beginning the letter, not with that information, but with something more positive). Still, it's so much fun to play with ordering material in this way that I encourage you to give it a try whenever you can.

Once you have made your plan, there are different ways you can write your assertion draft: You can read over your plan and your material, then just freewrite a new draft. Or you can take sections of your zero draft and move them into a new order, rewriting as necessary. Whichever you choose, make sure to get your picture of your reader—actual or imaginary—clear in your mind and *talk* to him or her on the page. Keep your attention focused on what you have to say to your reader and not on the words. Most of the time, when you do this, the words you need will appear. And, if they don't, you can always find exactly the right ones later.

When you are finished, make sure to take a break. You need some time away from your piece so that you can come back and see it with fresh eyes. Now it's time to ensure you have made yourself entirely clear to your readers: It's time to revise.

STEP 7: CLARIFY

Most people have a mistaken notion of what revising entails: They usually think that it means getting the words right. So they begin at the first sentence of their draft, try to fix it, move on to the second sentence, try to fix that one, and so on until their time or their patience is exhausted. This is an extremely inefficient way to revise, for revision is much more than mere editing. For functional writing (in school or at work), revision primarily involves making sure that you have said what you intended to say and that you have communicated your meaning clearly to your intended audience. It's certainly worthwhile to look at sentence structure and word choice, and to eliminate grammatical errors and spelling mistakes, but that part of revising needs to come later.

Revision, like the writing process itself, works much better if you do it in stages rather than all at once. One way to visualize those stages is to think of them as set out in an inverted triangle, with the widest part at the top. In that top part is the most important thing to look at when you revise: content. At the bottom are the less important things like grammar and spelling.

An image I like to use for the process of revision is that of a rack holding different pairs of eyeglasses; each pair enables you to look at one thing, and one thing only, in your writing. So each time you come back and read over your draft, it's as if you are putting on one particular pair of glasses, which gives you a particular kind of vision. Revision is, literally, re-vision, re-seeing; this approach enables you to see one thing at a time. Of course to use this approach, you have to be willing to read over your writing multiple times—something that many people struggle to do. If this is the case for you, see if you can overcome your reluctance; it's impossible to write well if you can't reread your work. And, after all, wouldn't you rather fix any problems that might exist *before* you give your work to a reader? Revision isn't really all that hard; you just have to know how to do it.

One thing that helps a lot in revising is to get some distance from your work before you come back to it. When you've just finished writing something, you can be so connected to it that it's hard to see it clearly. It's a good idea to plan for this time away from your work.

When you return to your writing, put on the pair of imaginary glasses that lets you see its content. Read over your draft for content alone, and from your own point of view as a writer. Ask yourself, *Is this piece saying what I want it to say? Have I left anything out?*

When you are satisfied that the piece as a whole is saying what you want it to say, you can look at the different parts of it—the paragraphs. Start by writing down at the top of a fresh piece of paper the main point you want your readers to get from your writing.[18] You should be able to summarize your point in a few sentences, at most. One way of thinking about this main point is that it is like a spine that goes all of the way through your piece, from the beginning to the end. *Everything* you say in your piece must connect to this main point, just as the ribs and shoulder and neck bones connect to the spine in our bodies. It's these connections that will help give your writing coherence.

To be sure that your piece of writing has coherence, continue the practice like this: Below your main point, draw a vertical line which divides your page into approximate halves. Now, read over your first paragraph and stop. In the left-hand margin of your page, write "P1" and then beside it, in one sentence, summarize what this paragraph is saying. You must write a complete sentence, with subject and verb, and your sentence must assert the point the paragraph is making, not simply describe what the paragraph is about. For instance, your summarizing sentence can't say, *This paragraph is about winter;* it must say something like, *Winter is beautiful* or *I hate winter,* or whatever your assertion may be. In the right-hand column, make notes to yourself about anything you need to do to revise this paragraph.

Repeat the process with the second paragraph, the third, the fourth, and so on through your piece.

Now you might be thinking, *I don't have time for this!* And it's true that this practice does take time ... however, it will teach you so much about how to create a coherent and powerful piece of writing that I think it's really worth finding the time to do it. And when you know that you can use this practice to revise, you will feel more comfortable spending less time on your earlier drafts. Eventually, if you use this practice enough, you'll be able to analyze each paragraph quickly, without having to write anything down.

When you analyze your paragraphs in this way, you might find that you intended a paragraph to be saying one thing, but in fact it's saying something else. You might discover that another paragraph has no point, or that it has more than one. (The guideline, as you probably know, is that each paragraph should have one main idea.) Perhaps you'll find that you're missing a necessary paragraph or two, or that you've repeated the same idea in more than one paragraph. While it's disconcerting to make these discoveries, it's far better to make them *before* you've given your writing to your readers—now you have time to rewrite the troublesome passages so that they make better sense.

Make sure, also, to look at the relationship between the summarizing sentences for each paragraph and the main point of your paper. Does each one connect to the main point? Have you made the connections clear?

You can also use the list of sentences you've created in this exercise to make sure that you've presented your ideas and information in an order that will make sense to your readers. Try this exercise: Imagine that you are someone else, someone who has never seen this piece of writing before. Then read slowly through your sentences from the exercise, and see if the second one makes sense after the first one, if the third one makes sense after the second one, and so on. If not, you may need to reorder your paragraphs.

You may also find that you need to add passages here and there in order to make better connections between two ideas. This kind of making connections is an essential part of writing (especially academic papers), and it can be difficult—not because of the writing, but because you have to *think* to create those connections. If you are in school, you may want to apply this technique of analyzing your paragraphs to your zero draft, rather than waiting until you've written an assertion draft. For what you end up with, after you've summarized each paragraph, is an outline—the most useful kind of outline, called a "conceptual outline," which gives you the skeleton of your piece. It gives you the bare bones of your ideas, stripped of all the word-flesh which can sometimes make you believe that you are being more clear than you actually are.

It's making sure that this skeleton is in place—that each bone of an idea or piece of information connects to the spine (main point), and that the bones are all in the right places—that is the most important thing you can do in revising most required writing. Functional writing doesn't have to be perfect. It doesn't even have to be great. It just has to be good enough. Most functional writing—a term paper, a report, what have you—is simply not worth agonizing over. It's a task; it has to get done. That's all. If you have something intelligent to say and have taken the time to consider your audience and purpose and to make sure you have communicated clearly, your audience will be happy. They're not looking for deathless prose; all they want is not to have to work too hard to understand what you're saying.

So while it's certainly possible to move on in revising to ordering and polishing every paragraph and sentence, to pondering every word and experimenting with different choices, for functional writing such care is largely a waste of time. (One exception would be a situation where you have used your own voice all the way through your assertion draft and now, once you've established your meaning, need to change some of the language to be more formal or to fit with the required style of a particular profession or academic discipline.) It is a good idea, though, to do a read-through for possible grammatical errors and to run a spell-check program; mechanical errors distract readers from what you have to say.

Reading through your "skeleton" as if you were someone else will give you practice in the most crucial skill for revision: being able to read your own words from a reader's point of view. Imagining a reader, putting yourself in his chair, and trying to read your draft through his eyes can also help you learn how to do this. So can reading your words aloud and listening to them as if you were someone else. Keep asking yourself, *Will this make sense to someone who isn't me?* One of the best ways to get answers to that question is, as one might guess, to find people with whom you can share your drafts. (If you'd like to learn how to do this, you'll find guidelines in chapter twelve.)

REQUIRED WRITING AS A PRACTICE (REPRISE)

Doing required writing can be very stressful: We *have* to do it; we may feel intimidated by our readers, especially if they are grading our work; and we have a deadline. One of the best ways to reduce the stress is to take charge of one's writing process. I hope the previous pages have given you some tools for doing that.

You may feel that this model of the writing process is a bit daunting in its complexity. Feel free to adapt it to your own needs. I have explained all the stages, so that you can have a clear picture of the entire process. But if you don't need to put a particular piece of writing through every step, then don't bother. I encourage you to see this approach not as fixed rules, but as a collection of tools you can use as you see fit.

Give yourself a chance to practice using these tools, and you will find that soon the process goes much more quickly than you expected. Like any other skills, developing ideas and communicating them on the page become easier with practice. Remember that these are new skills for you—you're *learning*—so be patient with yourself as you practice using them. You may find it helpful, once you've completed a project, to jot down a few notes about which tools you used and how they helped. If you let yourself practice, and learn, soon—probably sooner than you think—you will get to a place where you *know* you can communicate well on paper. Then doing required writing will no longer be a dreaded chore; perhaps it may even become a realm of growth for you, as you look for more challenging ways to exercise your writing skills.

Becoming a writer, as I have suggested in the earlier sections of this book, can be a relaxed, open-ended journey; required writing projects are finite and often fraught with anxiety and tension. That's in part because we feel that the results matter: We worry about how our writing at work will be received, or obsess about our grades. But it is possible to change our attitude toward required writing so that we don't focus on the immediate results, but instead on what we have learned as writers and on how a particular project has helped us take one more step on a writing path. Professional musicians often say that they perform best in concert when they imagine they're just practicing; writers, too, can adopt a new perspective toward required writing assignments, or performance writing tasks, and see them as simply more opportunities to practice.

SECTION 5
staying on the path

CHAPTER 18

Walking the Writer's Way

It is good to have an end to journey toward; but it is the journey that matters, in the end.

—Ursula K. Le Guin

So many people say they want to write; comparatively few of them actually do it. Why is that? The sense I get from many of my adult students is that—whether they actually voice the question or not—they are always asking: *Can I really do this?*

Adults who want to write often wonder: *Do I have any talent? Am I any good?* And so they create tests for themselves: They write a first short story and send it out, or they take a workshop and wait for the teacher's judgment on their work. They seem to believe that the ability to write is something a person either has or doesn't have, and they allow other people to make that determination. *If I can't do this well on my first try,* they seem to be saying to themselves, *then I'm obviously no good at it.* I think the main thing that keeps people from writing is that they assume that writing ability is something good writers are born with. This is just not true. You don't have to be born a writer; you can *become* one. Frances Mayes, author of *Under the Tuscan Sun,* taught writing to adults for many years; she says, "Many people find an interest in writing late; their talent is just waiting to be uncovered and developed."[19]

This idea that one can *become* a writer (rather than simply, miraculously, *being* one) can be difficult for some people to take in, especially for adults who have already achieved success in another field. It can be hard to let yourself start over again with writing. Many people bring high expectations to their writing: *I should be able to do this already.* It's essential to remember that, no matter what you have achieved in some other field, as a writer you are probably a beginner.

Rather than fighting this reality, and bringing expectations to your writing that will only defeat you, embrace your ignorance: Let yourself be a beginner. Let yourself *enjoy* being a beginner. Don't tell yourself, *I should be able to do this already;* instead, say, *Let me* learn *how to do this.*

To walk a writer's path is, as I hope I have made clear in this book, to be a learner. You don't have to have talent; you don't already have to be "good"; for that matter, you don't ever have to become "good." You need only two things: the desire to write and the willingness to put your time and energy into the process of learning and developing your skills.

Can I really do this?

Often when I hear that question from a workshop participant, it seems to mean, *Can I find a way to do this? What is the way to do this?*

There is no single way to be a writer; there are as many ways as there are writers. At the end of one workshop, Rachel had decided that what she needed next was simply to write in her journal. Gail had planned out a novel. Does this mean that Gail was "farther along" than Rachel? Absolutely not! They have different desires as writers; they walk different paths.

Some writers *must* travel; others hate to leave home. Some writers work best early in the morning; others wait until everyone else has gone to bed. Some writers began when they were five; others don't start until they've retired from their jobs at sixty-five. Trust your writer's intuition to help you find your own path, and don't give in to the temptation to compare your journey with anyone else's.

Can I really do this?

Sometimes what I hear in this question is: *Will I ever make any money at writing?*

I believe that there will always be work for people who know how to write well: jobs in public relations, fund-raising, and administration, for instance; or freelance writing and editing. (And other jobs too. Theo Epstein, general manager of the Red Sox, got his first job in baseball because of his excellent writing skills.) Some writers enjoy using their writing skills and getting paid for it. If you're planning to use your writing skills to support yourself, though, it's important to remember that writing will be your job. You might want to think about whether that's what you want; some people would rather save their writing energy for their own work.

Outside of such writing jobs, it's almost impossible to know whether you can ever make money with your writing. But don't fall into the trap of believing that if you are not making money, then you are not a "real" writer. The idea that the only real writers are the ones who make money from their work is just another myth. We live in a society where making money is the standard by which everything is judged: Can you make money at some activity? Well, then, it *must* be a good thing (even if it wrecks other people's lives, creates blights on the landscape, or pollutes the environment). You can choose to write, not for money, but for love. You can be an amateur rather than a professional writer.

To illuminate this idea of being an amateur writer, let's consider sports for a moment. Comparatively few people ever get to play a sport professionally and make money at it. But look at how many thousands—probably even millions—of people around the world play amateur sports or do sporting activities for recreation.

No one ever says to them, "If you're going to spend time skiing, or playing tennis or baseball, you *must* make money at it."

Few of us have the physical attributes to become professional athletes, but does that keep us from enjoying recreational sports or going to the gym? Why should writing be any different? Why shouldn't we make a place in our culture for amateur writers, just as we make a place for amateur sportsmen?

Writing can be something we do with our leisure time; just as amateur artists are "Sunday painters," so can we be "Saturday writers." What's wrong with that? Look at the kinds of things some people do with their free time: They play fantasy baseball, or they shop at the mall and then make another trip to return their purchases, or they watch television for hours upon hours. Why shouldn't you spend your recreation time writing, if that's what you want to do?

In the end, the real question is simple: How do you want to spend your time and your energy? If you discover that you love doing writing practice, than *do* it! Let yourself be a practicing rather than a performing or a professional writer. If writing makes you happy, if it gives you pleasure, then find ways to make time for it in your life.

Being an amateur rather than a professional writer may help you to concentrate on your learning rather than on results. Larry, one of my adult students commented in class one evening, "I'll never be a great tennis player, but that doesn't mean I can't take some lessons and learn how to play properly so I'll enjoy my games more. It's the same thing with writing: The more I learn, the more I enjoy doing it."

Can I really do this?

Sometimes it seems to me that this question means: *How can I find the time to write?*

Many years ago, a woman I knew went on a trip to Morocco. On her return, she told me of meeting a young Moroccan boy who

How to Be a Writer

was a shoemaker, as his father was, and as his grandfather had been before him. The boy said to her, "You Americans have too many choices." Today that statement rings even more true: Most of us live with an overwhelming array of choices in just about every area of life, from ice cream flavors to cable TV channels.

Like writing itself, being a writer is all about making choices: *Shall I sit down and write now? What do I want to work on today? Do I want to read this draft to somebody?*

Choosing to write often means choosing not to do something else. While we sometimes encounter people who seem blessed with boundless energy or independent means (or both), who seem able to have a family and a high-powered career *and* still find time to write, such people are rare. "Having it all" is a myth propagated by advertisers who want us to buy more things. If you want to spend some of your time writing, then you will probably have to choose not to do other things—go to the movies or do your laundry or visit your friends. This doesn't mean giving up such things entirely; it means, in any given moment, making the choice to write, or not.

One of the things establishing a writing practice will do for you is to give you a way to make these choices. I often have the sense that people who want to write believe that they must make a total commitment to writing, but they are afraid to do that because they're not sure writing is what they really want. But a commitment to writing doesn't have to happen all at once. Through your practice, you can *discover* what kind of relationship you want to have with writing. Life will keep offering you choices; you just have to keep making the choice to write—or not. Each step you take on your writing journey brings you further along your way. And then you get to choose again: *Do I want to write today? For how long?* There are always other claims on our time and energy; practicing writers are those who keep making the choice to write.

And if you keep making that choice, day after day, month after month, year after year, you will eventually discover that you have indeed made a commitment to your writing path. The exact nature of your commitment will depend on how you balance your need to write with the other demands on you. Perhaps you will fall passionately in love with writing and want to do it all the time. Or perhaps you will discover you don't *want* to write more than once a week or for more than an hour a day. As long as you are writing regularly, you are still a practicing writer, even if your practice looks very different from other people's. Find what works for you, right now, in your life. Perhaps later on your practice will be different. The real question—the only important question—is: *What place do you want writing to have in your life?* You can find out by doing the writing practices and seeing what happens.

And as you keep choosing to write, you may discover that other things become less important to you, that you don't need to go shopping as often or keep up with the latest movie releases. You may realize that you truly enjoy having a less busy life and decide to take other steps to keep it that way.

As a practicing writer you are entirely free to find your own writer's path. No one is forcing you to do it or expecting anything from you. Some people find this kind of freedom difficult to handle. Start small. See whether you can practice for ten minutes a few times a week and let yourself fully engage with it. Give yourself a little time afterwards for your subconscious to work. Notice what happens, how you feel, what you are thinking. Try it again. Getting yourself to sit down and write is a lot like getting yourself to the gym. At first you may have to push yourself past the inertia that has built up against doing the activity. But, soon, if you keep at it (and if you find you enjoy the activity), inertia will become momentum; you will want to keep returning to this activity that gives you pleasure. Writing then becomes, as my friend and fellow writer Dorothy puts it, not just something you want to do but something you *need* to do.

The freedom that comes with being a practicing writer seems to daunt some people. One woman I worked with was a recent dropout from the corporate world who had two master's degrees in completely different fields. She said she really wanted to write; but, having given herself the chance to do it, she couldn't. I suspect a lot of people are like this: They are so used to living their lives directed by others—parents or spouses or bosses or teachers—that they don't know how to live in an inner-directed way. I often think that it's not talent that many would-be writers lack, but the courage to pursue their own dreams, to live life according to their own needs and desires.

At the same time, remember that you can be realistic about your abilities and still take pleasure in using them. You can be realistic about the extent of your commitment to writing and still enjoy your practice. The journey, not the results, is what matters.

So, learn how to nurture yourself as a writer. Be like a good parent toward the part of your self that wants to write. It may be an eager, but easily daunted child, especially if it's never had any encouragement. Give it the support and encouragement it needs! Don't put pressure on, and at the same time, keep offering yourself new challenges: What do you want to learn about writing next? Remember that, above all, a practicing writer is a learner.

Don't obsess about a creating a perfect piece of writing. If you are dissatisfied with something you have written, don't give up. Ask yourself, *What have I learned here? How could I apply this to another piece of writing?* Cultivate your writer's intuition; ask it periodically, *What do I need to be learning now?* Remember that writing is a complex skill; there's a lot to be learned. Take your time. Learn at your own pace.

In t'ai chi practice, we often stop during the form to hold a particular posture. Peter, our teacher, will sometimes say, "Let yourself fully inhabit this step before you take the next one." I think this is excellent advice for walking a writer's path, too. Don't be in a rush to "get someplace" with your writing. Let yourself enjoy the place you are in now. Be patient. You've got your whole life to learn how be a writer. When you let yourself sink completely into each step on your writer's path, rather than rushing ahead to the next one, it will become clear to you what that next step needs to be, what you need to learn now.

And you don't have to do this learning only in solitude. In my workshops, we all do practices together. No one is required to share anything they've written, and few people do. What we do instead is talk about what happened as we did the practices: What we've noticed, what we've learned. Perhaps you might want to find a few like-minded folks and form your own writing practice group to get together once a week, do practices from this book (or of your own invention), and help each other learn. Such a group differs from the typical writers' group in that it is focused on practice rather than on developing particular pieces of writing. The whole purpose of a typical writers' group is to give and get responses to work-in-progress; to be part of such a group, you *must* be willing to share your work. But beginning or traumatized writers aren't ready to do that, and rightly so. They need a safe place where they can learn, at their own pace. Creating a writing practice group can give you the incentive to practice, as well as the companionship of other practicing writers, without the pressure to produce that the typical writers' group often creates.

Can I really do this?

Sometimes what I hear in this question is: *Will I ever be published?*

For many aspiring writers, getting published is the way to justify all the time and energy they put into writing, a way of telling themselves, and others, *I'm a real writer.* Once, at a writers' conference, a woman told me, "If I got published, then my daughter would stop expecting me to babysit for her instead of spending my time writing." And there's no doubt that seeing one's name in print is a genuine thrill. So, if getting published is essential to you, then by all means go for it.

At the same time, especially if you are just starting out on your path, you may want to adopt a different attitude toward getting published. What does that mean, anyway, to get published? What it means, at bottom, is to go public with your writing, to take it out of the privacy of your own practice and share it with others.

I see going public with one's work as a series of concentric circles, with the writer in the center. Perhaps, as you walk your path, you will feel that you want to share some of your writing with your partner, or with a close friend; you've brought some of your words into that first circle. Perhaps, a while later, you will decide to take a writing class or join a group where you read your words to others; that might be the next circle for you. Or perhaps you have a small party and invite friends to hear your new poems. Perhaps you'll decide to go to a writers' open mic and read your words to strangers (who might then become friends).

Going public with one's writing can be a natural impulse towards connection with others. If we write to communicate, we will want to reach others with what we have to say. The materials that come to us are gifts, and we can, in turn, give them to others. One way to begin to go public with writing is to think about someone who might appreciate and enjoy a gift of your thoughts on a particular subject. Write a letter or a poem or a story and give it to that person. (Many now-famous works of children's literature began as a gift from an adult to a child.)

One of my adult students once told me that he decided to take my writing workshop because he felt voiceless. "There's so much going on in the world," he said, "and I want to be able to say something about it." I sense that many people feel this way. Becoming a practicing writer can indeed help you educate yourself and develop a writing voice you like so that you feel confident in going public with your ideas. Perhaps you'll never have your own op-ed column, but you can write letters to the editor of your local newspaper. You can write letters to the CEOs of companies whose policies you object to; you can use your writing skills to support causes you believe in; you can write an article for your church newsletter; you can start a blog—when you think small about getting published, you'll discover lots of ways to get your words out into the world. And don't underestimate the power of such activities: Thoughtful, well-crafted writing can effect real change in the world.

Like everything else about writing, going public with our words is something we can practice. Start slowly, with people you trust. Perhaps eventually, as you become more comfortable with sharing your work, you will want to begin to send it out through conventional and new publishing channels. If you want to take that path, here are a few words of advice. If you decide to "go pro," if you want to compete with professionals in a particular writing market, then act like a professional. Respect and honor the craft of writing. Make sure your work is as good as you can possibly get it before you send it out. Do your homework and find the appropriate places to which to send your writing; don't waste agents' and editors' time. There's a lot to learn about the business of marketing your work, and many books and Web sites that can teach you what you need to know.

At the same time, I believe that writers need to take responsibility for the material we choose to put out into the world. There's a difference between private and public writing. In your practice writing you can say anything you like. But when you decide to make your material public, I believe that you have a responsibility to consider its possible effects on others. I urge you to think carefully about how your stories or poems or essays might affect your readers. Will they help people? Will they harm them in some way? Have a clear sense of your purpose in sending these particular pieces out into the world.

Sometimes the realization of responsibility toward one's readers takes beginning writers by surprise. One of my adult students once told a class that she used to read violent murder mysteries all the time. But then she began to plan her own novel. "I'm not having any gratuitous violence in *my* book!" she said.

Can I really do this?

There's another meaning to this unspoken question, I think: *Is it okay for me to do this thing I really want to do? Will people still love me?*

On the second night of a weekly writing workshop for adult beginners one woman said, "I love doing the freewriting practice, but it feels so *selfish* to be taking the time to write. I have a job, and a business partner, and a husband."

Is it selfish to spend time at the gym, working out, so that we can become stronger and healthier? Most of us would probably say no. Then why is it selfish to engage in writing practices that will strengthen other parts of us, like our imagination and our power of observation and our intellect (which are, one might argue, more important than our muscles)? Being able to imagine more fully or observe more carefully or think more clearly can do just as much for your well-being and the quality of your life as physical exercise. Just like working out, exercising your writer's powers makes you feel alive, and keeps you alive. Brain scientists now know that mental exercise is the key to keeping our brains fit for our entire lives. Writing practice provides us with this kind of exercise.

A writing practice can make you a more interesting and fulfilled human being even if you never publish a thing. Is that selfish? Using powers other than the intellect (which most of us must use at work or in school) can give you mental balance; learning to observe can lead you to be more fully present in the world, less "in your head"; strengthening your imagination or your curiosity might give you new ways of doing familiar activities or lead you into unexpected areas of interest and excitement—you'll have new things to think and talk about. Your practice time can be your time to *play*, a time that can relax and refresh you mentally, emotionally, and spiritually. (And, as my students always say, "It's just so much *fun* to use your powers!") As you exercise your powers during this playtime, you can develop a sense of who you are that doesn't depend on how you look or how much money you make. One of my adult students said, at the end of a workshop, "Writing practice has given me a new way to live my life. Now I will try doing something just to see what happens. I could never do that before. I've become much braver."

When you exercise your powers, your life can indeed be transformed. And using those powers, through writing or otherwise, can make a difference in other people's lives, too. When you spend your time doing something you love to do, you become a happier person, whose happiness can warm those around you.

Can I really do this?

Over time, if you continue your writing practice, you may discover a dedication to it, to your own work, that you may not have previously experienced. If "work" has always been for you something that you *have* to do, you may, for the first time, discover the joy of doing work you love. Your practice may become, as any practice can, a spiritual practice, giving you a home from which to venture into the world and to which you can always return. Your practice may become a kind of sacred time, a ritual which grounds and centers you every day, and which you value for its own sake, not because of what you produce. A writing practice can give you a place to root yourself, invaluable in this time when so many of us are forced by our jobs to uproot and move every few years. And while writing practice is indeed a powerful way to develop your writing skills, you may come to value it not (or not only) as a way to become a better writer, but as an end in itself. If you choose to dedicate yourself fully to your practice—by which I mean you do it regularly and faithfully—it can transform your life.

For me, a dedication to writing practice is a giving of one's self to the practice and to the learning. It's a kind of love. And, like any spiritual practice, it can, over time, become a cleansing fire that burns away everything about us that is not essential and leaves only our true selves to shine out, illuminating our own paths and even casting light into the lives of others.

So ultimately it doesn't matter where you arrive as a writer; what matters is the journey, the taking of one step after another in such a way that you can participate fully in that step, and appreciate and enjoy every one. This doesn't mean that every step will be easy; becoming a writer, like doing anything else worthwhile, is hard work at times. Learning how to do new things can be frustrating. But learning how to do new things is also what keeps us awake, what keeps us alive to the worlds within us and the worlds without.

For in the end, being a practicing writer is a wonderful way to live: to live slow, to live simple, to live deep.

Remember that it can take time to find your path. You may have to wander for a while, ending up in some blind alleys, perhaps, or at the edge of a precipice from which you have to backtrack. But eventually, if you keep practicing, you will find the subjects that call to you, you will find your voice, and you will develop the skills that enable you to walk your own writer's way. So I urge you to have patience; to persevere, no matter what difficulties beset you; and to remember the words of Sir Winston Churchill: *Never, ever, ever give up.*

Can I really do this?

Yes, you can.

Enjoy your journey. May peace attend you.

While you will probably spend most of your practice time by yourself, you may also sometimes want to get together with others to practice. You can practice with just one other person or in a group; if you already belong to a writers' group, you can make practice sessions part of your meetings. When you practice with others you may find that there's a particular kind of energy that gets generated by several people all concentrating on the same task; that energy can fuel everyone's practicing. Here are some guidelines:

1. Make sure that everyone understands the basic idea of learning through practice, and that there is no pressure to share what you write in an exercise. (Sometimes, after a practice, people will want to share what they have written, but no one should feel that sharing is required.)

2. After you do a practice, give everyone a few minutes to reflect on paper about what they noticed in doing it. Then discuss what happened. Be respectful of other people's experiences: Different people may do the practices differently, take them in different directions, and you can get good ideas from them that will enliven your own practice.

3. Try practices from this book, and encourage everyone to invent their own exercises as well. Often a discussion of what happened during one practice will spark an idea for a new one..

4. At the end of the practice session, give everyone a few minutes to write down an answer to this question: What did you learn today that you can apply to your own practice or to a piece you are working on?

How to Be a Writer

Writer's Bookshelf: Some Books for Further Reading

There are hundreds of writing books available, and I urge you to discover the ones that speak to you. Here is a list of some of my favorites (as well as a few other related books):

Joan Aiken. *The Way to Write for Children: An Introduction to the Craft of Writing Children's Literature.* New York: St. Martin's Press, 1982.

Marion Dane Bauer. *What's Your Story? A Young Person's Guide to Writing Fiction.* New York: Clarion Books, 1992.

Ray Bradbury. *Zen in the Art of Writing: Releasing the Creative Genius Within You.* New York: Bantam, 1992.

Joseph Bruchac. *Our Stories Remember: American Indian History, Culture, and Values through Storytelling.* Golden, CO: Fulcrum Publishing, 2003.

Tell Me a Tale: A Book about Storytelling. New York: Harcourt Brace, 1997.

John Carey. *Eyewitness to History.* New York: Harper, 1997.

Peter Elbow. *Writing with Power: Techniques for Mastering the Writing Process.* New York: Oxford University Press, 1981

Rudolf Flesh. *The Art of Readable Writing.* New York, Harper & Row, 1949.

Ralph Fletcher. *A Writer's Notebook: Unlocking the Writer Within You.* New York: Avon Books, 1996.

Jon Franklin. *Writing for Story: Craft Secrets of Dramatic Nonfiction.* New York: Penguin Books, 1986

Brewster Ghiselin. *The Creative Process.* Berkeley: University of California Press, 1985.

Temple Grandin and Catherine Johnson. *Animals in Translation.* New York: Scribner, 2005.

Ted Hughes. *Poetry in the Making.* New York: Faber and Faber, 1967.

Stephen King. *On Writing: A Memoir of the Craft.* New York: Scribner, 2000.

Damon Knight. *Creating Short Fiction: The Classic Guide to Writing Short Fiction.* Cincinnati, OH: Writer's Digest Books, 1981.

Ursula K. Le Guin. *Steering the Craft: Exercises and Discussion on Story Writing for the Lone Navigator or the Mutinous Crew.* Portland, OR: The Eighth Mountain Press, 1998.

Betsy Lerner. *The Forest for the Trees: An Editor's Advice to Writers.* New York: Riverhead, 2001.

Richard Marius. *A Writer's Companion.* New York: McGraw-Hill, 1998.

Frances Mayes. *The Discovery of Poetry: A Field Guide to Reading and Writing Poems.* New York: Harcourt, 2001.

Richard Restak, M.D. *Mozart's Brain and the Fighter Pilot: Unleashing Your Brain's Potential.* New York: Three Rivers Press, 2001.

Robert and Michele Root-Bernstein. *Sparks of Genius: The 13 Thinking Tools of the World's Most Creative People.* Boston: Houghton Mifflin, 1999.

William Stafford. *Writing the Australian Crawl: Views on the Writer's Vocation.* Ann Arbor: University of Michigan Press, 1978.

Studs Terkel. *The Good War: An Oral History of World War II.* New York: Pantheon, 1984.

Brenda Ueland. *If You Want to Write.* St. Paul, MN: Greywolf Press, 1987.

Jane Yolen. *Take Joy: A Writer's Guide to Loving the Craft.* Cincinnati, OH: Writer's Digest Books, 2006.

Marilee Zdenek. *The Right-Brain Experience.* New York: McGraw-Hill, 1983.

William Zinsser. *On Writing Well: The Classic Guide to Writing Nonfiction, 30th anniversary edition.* New York: Harper, 2006.

How to Be a Writer

Notes

When complete details on sources are not given here, they can be found in *A Writer's Bookshelf*.

CHAPTER 1

1 *usually called freewriting*
I learned this practice from Peter Elbow's *Writing with Power*.

CHAPTER 2

2 *Writer and filmmaker Woody Allen*
From Betsy Lerner, *The Forest for the Trees: an editor's advice to writers* [New York: Riverhead, 2001, 37].

CHAPTER 3

3 *"A writer is not so much someone who has something to say..."*
William Stafford, *Writing the Australian Crawl*, 117.

CHAPTER 6

4 *"to see a World"*
William Blake, "Auguries of Innocence."

CHAPTER 7

5 *today government*
Temple Grandin, *Animals in Translation*, 27.

6 *Many recent studies have demonstrated*

For these and other studies, see the articles and bibliographies at *www.easytoremember.com* and *www.turnoffyourtv.com.*

7 *The average unimaginative*
Richard de Mille, *Put Your Mother on the Ceiling,* 17. In 1999 the Kaiser Family Foundation study reported that "American youth spend more time with media than with any single activity other than sleeping." Of particular concern to many parents and educators is the violent content of so many television programs, movies, and videos. A recent study by the Parents Television Council *(http://www.parentstv.org/PTc/publications/reports/stateindustryviolence/exsummary.asp)* reported that "violence on the six major television networks increased in every time slot between 1998 and 2002." By the time most children have finished elementary school, they will have watched eight thousand murders on TV. By the time they are eighteen, they will have witnessed more than *two hundred thousand* violent acts on TV, including forty thousand murders. *(http://www.csun edu/science/health/docs/tv&health.htm.)*

CHAPTER 8

8 *The novelist Louis Bromfield*
From Rudoph Flesch, *The Art of Readable Writing,* 50.

CHAPTER 10

9 *You have been in Afghanistan*
Sir Arthur Conan Doyle, "A Study in Scarlet," *Sherlock Holmes: The Complete Novels and Stories, Vol. 1* [New York: Bantam, 2003, 7].

10 *sandwiched between*
Sir Arthur Conan Doyle, "A Scandal in Bohemia," *Sherlock Holmes: The Complete Novels and Stories, Vol. 1,* 246.

CHAPTER 11

11 *the poet Stanley Kunitz*
Bill Moyers, *Fooling with Words, A Celebration of Poets and their Craft* [New York, William Morrow, 1999, 91].

How to Be a Writer

CHAPTER 12

12 *movies of your reader's mind*

Peter Elbow's approach to getting response from readers (which I have used in classes for years and draw on here) is described in his books, *Writing without Teachers* and *Writing with Power*.

CHAPTER 13

13 *And after all, it is not the expectation*

Jane Yolen, *Favorite Folktales from Around the World*, 35 .

14 *Even if a narrative*

Ursula LeGuin, *Steering the Craft, xii.*

CHAPTER 14

15 *The ontological relativity*

Felix Guattari, quoted by Alan Sokal and Jean Bricmont, *Fashionable Nonsense: Postmodern Intellectuals' Abuse of Science* [Picador, 1999, 167].

16 *Our complex*

Jean Baudrillard, quoted by Sokal and Bricmont, 153.

CHAPTER 17

17 *After you've read through*

I learned this technique, and the "safe audience" exercise, from Peter Elbow's *Writing with Power.*

18 *Start by writing down*

I have adapted this exercise from one described by Marie Ponsot and Rosemary Deen, *Beat Not the Poor Desk* [Portsmouth, NH: Boynton-Cook, 1989].

CHAPTER 18

19 *Many people find*

From Mayes, *The Discovery of Poetry,* page *xviii.*

Acknowledgments

This book had its beginnings twenty-five years ago, when I first began teaching writing. I would come home after a class, my mind buzzing with ideas: what went well, what didn't go well, what I might do differently next time. I got into the habit of writing down these thoughts; and as I wrote, new ideas came to me about teaching and about learning. Gradually, as the years went by, my ideas shaped and reshaped themselves into the form they have taken in this book.

But even though the book is now finished, the processes of writing, teaching, and learning continue to fascinate me, and my ideas about them continue to grow. So I am pleased that the existence of the Internet gives me the opportunity to share new ideas (or new takes on old ones) at www.wherewriterslearn.com. I hope you will visit for free additional writing lessons or to comment on the book.

As all teachers do, I have learned much from others. My most important debt is to the work of Peter Elbow, whose *Writing with Power* set me on my own learning and writing path. Other books, their titles long since forgotten, gave me ideas for things to try out in class, as did instructors in writing workshops I attended. I hope anyone I have neglected to credit in these notes will forgive my lapse of memory.

I am most grateful to my students—especially those at Harvard Divinity School and The Cambridge Center for Adult Education. Their enthusiasm for my approach helped me decide that I needed to write this book; their questions made me think harder about how to write it. I am also grateful to the various deans at HDS who supported my work there, especially Jane Smith, Clarissa Atkinson, Susan Beth Dunton, and Tim Whelsky, and to Alison Streit and Charlotte Silver at CCAE for hiring me to teach writing workshops and inviting me to participate in CCAE's annual writers' conference.

I appreciate the support I have gotten for this project from my friends and fellow writers, especially Dorothy Stephens and Rachel Hyde. My special thanks to my longtime friend, Tom Hallock, associate publisher and director of sales and marketing at Beacon Press, for his sound advice on the business side of book making. I extend deep appreciation to my friend, freelance editor Heidi Hill, who read several drafts of the book, offering helpful suggestions each time, and who also collaborated with me on editing the manuscript.

This book would not be in your hands now without the efforts of the Writer's Digest editorial, art, and sales and marketing teams. I am indeed grateful for all their hard work.

Finally, I have been blessed with the opportunity to learn from two extraordinary teachers, Betta van der Kolk and Peter Wayne. Though I never discussed any of the book with them, their teaching and support helped make it possible.

Index

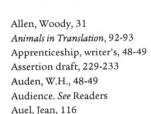